THE BLUE JELLYBEAN, HEDY LAMARR, AND WE DON'T EAT NEGROES
†

A Memoir

I0142913

by

BISHOP KARL PRÜTER

The Borgo Press
An Imprint of Wildside Press

MMVII

CONTENTS
†

Preface 5

Chapter 1: My Family 9
Chapter 2: Schools and Jobs in the Depression 19
Chapter 3: School Strike and the Oxford
    Movement 31
Chapter 4: Northeastern University 43
Chapter 5: The Lutheran Theological Seminary.... 57
Chapter 6: Maine.. 67
Chapter 7: Orford and Orfordville 79
Chapter 8: In and Around the Connecticut
    Valley 93
Chapter 9: Berwyn 103
Chapter 10: Maywood and Itasca........................ 117
Chapter 11: Bavaria, Boston, and Zuni................ 125
Chapter 12: Granville Avenue, Chicago 139
Chapter 13: The Ozarks 153

About the Author... 166

PREFACE
†

Although I have lived eighty-six years and my wife insists I must live another thirty, the time has come to put down in paper where I have been and what it all means. This book thus represents my memoirs, and as such it is about many things. First, it is about my life growing up in a working class family, getting an education, establishing a career in the ministry, building a career in teaching, finding and marrying a life partner, creating a family, and writing and publishing a body of works on religion. In short this book is about making my life in America.

Along the way, I have worked in a great variety of jobs, which brought me into contact with some of the most intriguing job situations and fascinating work colleagues and supervisors. During this same lifetime, I have moved from the religion I grew up in, Lutheranism, to involvement in Moral Re-armament, to Congregationalism, to finally the Old Catholic movement, and these memoirs discuss and explain my move to each religious stage of my career. In one sense I never made dramatic changes in my religious direction, because in each tradition I took what seemed true and valuable to establishing one's relationship to God. They all had something to offer, and they helped me arrive to my present understating of a good Christian.

But this book is not only about me. It is about my family and about the people I have met and have known. The family I grew up in like most families had its share of disputes and interesting and even eccentric characters, and as a child this extended family environment is where one first learns about the world, and takes lifelong lessons from the experience. Then, there is nothing like raising a family that can bring more joy and at the same time difficulties, and the experience allowed me to avoid some of the pitfalls one saw in the family from which I was raised. While the events and incidents that arose with my children may appear to be of only the particular interest to this parent they often resonate with universal relevance. In short, we all have been there.

Finally, in my movements over the decades from Allentown, Pennsylvania; New York; Boston; Philadelphia; Maine; New Hampshire; Chicago; Bavaria; Boston and New Hampshire again; New Mexico; and the Ozarks in southern Missouri, I had the opportunity to see and observe the local habits and customs of people in all their infinite variety. In the following pages, I offer stories on these people, whose personalities and idiosyncrasies readers may have similarly encountered in people they have known.

By being unique individuals we all have a unique life to tell, but I hope the reader comes away from these pages having learned something beyond the particulars of my life to something more general about human nature, the raising of families, the way one earns a living, and the directions one takes in his or her relationship with God.

I am very grateful to the many people who contributed to *My Lives*. First of all, I am most thankful to my son, Robert, who spent many hours in editing and organizing my unorganized jottings into a chapter by chapter narrative. All of my seven children have contributed much, sometimes in just supplying a name or an incident that I had forgotten, other times suggesting the direction the book should take. So thank you Nancy, Karl, Maurice, and Kathy. In their own way Hugo and Stephen, who are no longer with us, have also made their contribution. We are a family.

—Bishop Karl Prüter
Highlandville, Missouri

CHAPTER ONE
†
MY FAMILY

"My mother called me 'Hughie'..."

I was born and christened, "Hugo Rehling Strongmiller." My birth certificate said I was the male child of Hugo Strongmiller and Katherine Rehling, born July 3, 1920. Growing up my mother and my relatives all called me "Hughie," which I accepted without protest. When I was old enough to go to school, the teachers insisted on calling me "Hugo." It was a name that in America was a hard one to have. Children would tease me by saying such things as "You go there" or "Where do you go?" If they were my size I stopped the teasing with a punch or two. I must have been a bit large for my age because I usually was able to put an end to the teasing. Having to fight over the name made me quite determined that I would be called "Hugo" with a measure of respect. Of course, my mother called me "Hughie" all of her eighty-two years of her life. When I was in sixth grade I had a friend, Jim Ryan, who called me "Hughie," and when I told him never to do it, he pointed out that my mother called me "Hughie." I replied, "I would never punch my mother in the nose, but if you called me "Hughie" one more time that is what I shall do to you."

Jim Ryan had no other friends. I think I only became a friend to him for that reason. Everyone 1 thought is entitled to have, at least, one friend. Jim and his family lived differently than my family and I. One day I was invited to have lunch with the Ryans and was surprised that their lunch consisted of a sandwich and a glass of milk. When they didn't offer me more that just one sandwich, it seemed strange to me. In my home at noontime we usually had two or three sandwiches. For many years, I had the same sandwich made of rye bread and summer bologna. I was often sent to Woolworth's delicatessen counter to buy a pound of summer bologna, which for many years was priced at twenty cents a pound.

I had to spend my first few years with my uncle, Maurice (pronounced "Morris"), in Pennsylvania Dutch country. As a child I was bilingual, speaking English and a German dialect known as Pennsylvania Dutch. Uncle Maurice was an intriguing man and I learned much from him. He, like most of his neighbors worked in the silk mills as a weaver. When the Depression struck wages plummeted to an average of eight dollars a week.

My uncle became active in the union movement and was soon blackballed by management. He kept up his union activities but had to earn his living in a great variety of ways. He bought a truck and became a fruit and vegetable huckster. He did well and seemed to enjoy the work. He did that for a few years and then turned to bootlegging. No, it had nothing to do with liquor but with coal. Many of the mines were shut down and thousands of miners were unemployed. Since there was no work to be had, many of the unemployed miners began to mine coal in the closed mines. The owners raised no objection since it hardly seemed like the correct thing to do. The owners were not mining the coal, so why shouldn't those who are willing and able be permitted to do so? They found a ready market and soon people like Uncle Maurice bought trucks and bought the coal that was being mined. They hauled it to New York City and sold it at a competitive price. A reader may ask, "Wasn't it stolen coal? Why weren't they prosecuted?" During the Depression some things were overlooked and even encouraged. As far as the bootleggers were concerned they proudly advertised what they were doing. Many had signs on their trucks that clearly stated what they were doing. Uncle Maurice had one that read as follows:

LEHIGH VALLEY BOOTLEG
COAL ASSOCIATION
Fullerton, PA, Enterprise 905

Uncle Maurice enjoyed the work although he spent many days fixing his Dodge truck. Going into the Appalachian Mountains and coming out of the Lehigh Valley laden with coal wreaked havoc on the truck. It was a marginal living, at best, but my uncle enjoyed it. He entertained the family with many stories concerning his visit to the Big Apple. They had to approach people they didn't know and sell them coal. They had two things going for them. First was price. They bought the coal from miners who had small overhead. No taxes to pay on the mine property, and sadly, few safety measures in the mines they entered. Another sales argument they offered was that the coal was hand cracked rather than cracked by machinery. This gave the coal a different sheen and it was said that machine cracking let out the beneficial gas found naturally in coal.

Word got around that the bootleggers offered good coal at a good price. One Italian neighbor approached Uncle Maurice and suggested he call upon a friend of his in New York's Italian neighborhood. To help the sale to go smoothly he suggested that Uncle Maurice take his son along. The son would enjoy the adventure of the trip and feel he was being useful. The son did enjoy the trip but when they called on his father's friend they ran into difficulty. My uncle introduced the boy as Tony's son and immediately the man spoke to the boy in Italian. Unfortunately the boy didn't speak Italian. Immediately the prospect felt they were trying to con him. He said, "The boy no speaka Italian. He can't be Tony's son." It took a long and difficult discussion before the man would agree to buy the coal.

It was a long and tiring trip and when the bootleggers unloaded their trucks they wanted to find a place to eat. Since they were usually in unfamiliar and different neighborhoods the question frequently came up. "Where should we eat?" One day one of the drivers answered by saying he saw a place nearby. "Is it expensive?" he was asked. "Naw," he said, "it's a little place in a cellar." So the driver who discovered the basement restaurant led the way and the three other truck drivers followed. When they arrived they took the stairway down into the restaurant and were surprised to see about twenty tables with linen tablecloths and set with plates and silverware. From a restaurant's standpoint they made a frightful group as they were covered with coal dust from unloading their trucks. But a waiter well attired came and took their orders. As he left for the kitchen a five-piece orchestra came and began to play for them. At that point they were sure this was not going to be an inexpensive meal and that the whole situation was incongruous. Probably it was the incongruity of the situation that decided them to stay. It was a story that they knew they would often repeat to the folks back in Pennsylvania.

Uncle Maurice's next job took him to more familiar territory. The Depression was letting up a bit and his blacklisted days were behind him. He heard about a silk mill that was looking for a pattern weaver. Although he had years of silk weaving experience behind him he had never been a pattern weaver. Nevertheless, he applied for the job and when he was asked if he was experienced he claimed ten years experience. However, he wasn't specific about what he had been doing. After his interview he was taken into the plant and brought to the particular loom he was supposed to use. He eyeballed it a bit and noticed that there were three levers, which he assumed he was expected to know what to do with them. He didn't have any idea. There was a man working on a loom to his right and one working on a loom to his left. His gut instinct told him the man on the right might be a "squealer," so he turned to the man on his left and approached him with these words. "The last place I worked the loom only had two levers. How does this one work?" The weaver nodded and said, "Yeah some do. Let me show you." Ergo, Uncle Maurice now became a pattern weaver. As his young nephew I listened in awe and remembered it years later when I applied for a job as a boys' worker and was specifically asked if I could teach basketball. I gave an Uncle Maurice kind of answer saying that at my previous job I had to handle "all the activities."

My mother's family was large. She had two brothers and five sisters. They lived in and near Allentown, Pennsylvania. They visited often and my mother, dad, and I often drove to Pennsylvania to see them. Unfortunately there were constant arguments that never seemed to cease. They were never over anything big, but if we visited and went to one sister or brother first some of the others would become angry. Since they all didn't live in the same house, we had to visit someone first. Even as a child I could see and understand that. But the arguments went on and on. The sisters were all avid gardeners and exchanged plants, plant bulbs, and seeds constantly. Unfortunately, whenever one sister gave some of these things to the others, one or more sisters felt she had been more generous to the others than to them.

My mother and her relatives was always finding something to fight about and get angry with each other—no matter how miniscule the slight—which I think helped me to grow up into a more harmonious person. When I was in school and my cousin Fred was also in school many of our family members would say, "Everyone in our family works

except for Fred and Hugo. They are the only bums."
It didn't cause me anger, only amusement.

As a child I enjoyed my aunts and uncles. I
had a favorite and she was Aunt Amelia. I don't remember why. I also remember many incidents that
brought me pleasure, insight into human nature, and
sometimes amusement. One incident says so much
about the family. Aunt Blanche and Uncle Truman
were quite thrifty and managed to live well on what
Uncle Truman earned. They bought an old barbershop and had it towed to a lot they purchased near
the Allentown Airport and Uncle Maurice proceeded to remodel the barbershop and make a very
nice house for them. Being as thrifty as they were
they told Uncle Maurice they did not need a bath-
room but would settle for an outhouse. They said
they had always used one and that an inside toilet
was an unnecessary expense.

Aunt Helen liked the idea of a house by the
airport and wanted to be near her sister, and so
moved to a house near the airport. But she didn't
feel she could afford an inside toilet and Uncle
Maurice build her an outhouse. Aunt Helen never
had any money. Her husband, Raymond, was not a
good provider and they never learned to manage
what they had. Maybe, also misfortune had a way of
following them. One time they inherited four hundred dollars from Uncle Raymond's mother and
they bought a car. Two weeks later they wrecked
the car. Aunt Blanche on the other hand could have
bought a car but felt they couldn't afford one.

One time when Aunt Helen and Uncle Raymond came for a visit I received an understanding
concerning the different financial situation between

the two aunts. Uncle Raymond and Aunt Helen had gone sightseeing and my mother was sitting on the couch in the living room with copious tears coming down her cheeks. I immediately asked, "What is wrong?" Then I realized my mother's tears were caused by her laughter. She tried to tell me what was causing this laughter, but she had difficulty getting out the words she needed to tell the story.

Between all her laughter this story took her at least an hour to tell. "Well, Hughie, you know that both Aunt Blanche and Aunt Helen have outhouses." That revealing statement was followed by at least ten minutes of laughter. "Well a few months ago Aunt Helen's outhouse was pretty near full [more laughter], and then [more laughter] a 'honey dipper' [a person who cleans out outhouses] came by and asked if she needed him. She said, "Yes, and what will it cost?" They talked a bit and it was agreed that for forty dollars he would do the job.

Then came a flood of laughter and tears. Finally she started in again. "A few weeks later two farmers came to Aunt Blanche's house and said they noticed the outhouse [more laughter]. They wanted to buy the contents of her outhouse to be used as manure and they actually paid Aunt Blanche twenty-five dollars. Aunt Helen said it was crazy, that Aunt Blanche had more money than she did. She said, 'I have nothing. It cost me forty dollars to get my outhouse cleaned out. And Blanche is able to sell her own shit'." That really got the water works going. Mother struggled to go on. "Helen told me that she did not know why she had to pay to have her outhouse cleaned and Blanche could sell her *shit*! Aunt Helen said she often went to the grocery store and met Aunt Blanche and she said, 'I've looked in her grocery basket and she doesn't buy any better food than I do. Tell me, Katherine, why I have to pay to have my shit hauled away and she can sell hers for twenty five dollars?'" By the time mother got the whole story out I was almost laughing as much as she did.

My mother kept close contact with her family. Many years later Aunt Helen got a divorce from Uncle Raymond and for several years made her own way working in the silk mills. Then she met Frank who was as colorful a character as eastern Pennsylvania had to offer. He was a retired railroad man and drew a good pension. He also was a practicing pow-wow doctor. To those not from eastern Pennsylvania, a pow-wow doctor needs an explanation. In that region one can buy the *Six and Seventh Books of Moses*, a book filled with prayers and chants that reputedly can be used to cure any and all diseases known to mankind. Pow-wow doctors are just like regular physicians. Most regular physicians work on a fee by call basis. The fee is paid whether you get better or not. Pow-wow doctors did well back then and Uncle Frank was successful at it.

When Aunt Helen married Uncle Frank, he had retired, except occasionally to help out a friend or a relative. My mother swore that Uncle Frank healed her sore knee. Uncle Frank was heavy set and in his elderly years was not very steady on his feet. Aunt Helen was able to manage but she asked mother to come live with them as she said she could use mother's help. By the way, this was a new Aunt Helen. She used to swear like a sailor, but Uncle Frank did not approve of foul language so she no longer swore. First, she liked Uncle Frank and secondly he took very good care of her. Each year he bought her a new Packard and almost anything else she wanted. She, Uncle Frank, and Aunt Helen's dog "Bitsy" lived a peaceful and uneventful life.

My mother was an avid letter writer and although her English was not the best I looked forward to receiving her many letters. I remember one in particular because her letters were often a bit cryptic. The following lines were unforgettable. "Frank is finding it harder and harder to walk. He uses a cane, but yesterday he fell on Aunt Helen's dog. No more dog!"

CHAPTER TWO
†
SCHOOLS AND JOBS IN THE DEPRESSION

"On LaGrange Avenue is where I learned even a kid could earn money."

When I was seven years old my mother decided that she was able to have me live with her. She was working as a housekeeper for the Morris Rosen family in Poughkeepsie, New York. She lived in one room in the attic of the Rosen house and I would share it with her for the next two years. It was a wonderful place to live. The house had a number of bookcases and I found them to be a treasure. During those two years I can't remember all the books I read, but two in particular drew my attention: *The History of France* and *The History of Russia*. Thus began my life long love of history.

The first year with mother she sent me to St. Mary's Elementary School. The choice was made because I had attended Catholic school while at Uncle Maurice's, and she received the indoctrination that the public schools were inferior. I did well at school and they fed my avid appetite for reading. I would get daily reading assignments and was told to ask my mother to help me. Unfortunately when my mother asked me about my assignments I inflated them. The nun had assigned maybe two stories, but I would always add two or three more. My mother felt the assignments were much too long and decided the following year to send me to public school, which she felt would be more reasonable. Since I didn't get any reading assignments in public school I didn't have any to inflate.

However, it was there that I met my first love, Nancy Hughes. What attracted her to me was that she had very white skin. She might have been anemic but I used to walk her home, which at that age was a big deal. While Nancy had my attention my mother met Wilhelm Pruter and I soon would have a stepfather. I did not know my biological father and was told that he was dead. I am sure that one time he visited mother and was introduced to me as my uncle. I was playing with a game and my "uncle" observed me but we didn't talk.

The Rosens were the paragons of thrift. When the electric record player was invented and put on the market the Rosens didn't rush out to buy one but they had their Victrola converted. They did the same with the invention of the refrigerator. They kept the old icebox, but had a motor put in the basement and ran a copper pipe up to the icebox so that where the ice chest used to be there were now coils that cooled the icebox and the ice trays. The iceman was no longer needed and I recall talking with him, because I and the other children in the neighborhood always met him so that he could cut some pieces of ice for us. He said it was too bad we weren't getting ice from him, because refrigerated ice was not good for us, and we should stick to *natural ice*. In fact shortly after his truck displayed a sign proclaiming that they offered natural ice. Of course it was a losing battle. Especially since everyone knew the ice came from the Hudson River, which was the same river into which we dumped our sewage. Eventually, it became so bad that all the Sturgeon and the Shad, the principal fish in the river, disappeared. It was decades later that the river was cleaned and the game fish returned.

Mother and Wilhelm Pruter didn't have a long courtship, and one night I was informed that they had gotten married and we would soon be leaving Poughkeepsie, and moving to nearby New Hamburg where my stepfather worked. From day one, he was Dad. I don't think I ever mentioned to anyone that he was my step dad. He was a real father to me and the only "Dad" that I have ever known.

Living in New Hamburg was a wonderful experience. Dad worked as a factory foreman and the factory and the house we lived in were on a fifty-four acre estate. The house was frame and six stories high. The ground floor was huge, but each additional floor was smaller and the sixth consisted of only one room. It was quite old and went back to the whaling days and apparently the original owner was lost at sea on a whale hunt. Therefore there was a widow's walk. The first floor was occupied by Mr. and Mr. Northrop, the owners of the estate. We had an apartment on the second floor, and on the third floor lived Mr. Northrop's sister, Bessie.

Some distance away was a small factory, which made carbon brushes, which were sold to car manufacturers and car-parts dealers. I was told that Mr. Northrop was the inventor of the carbon brush, which was needed for the starter motors and the generators.

There were three other buildings on the estate. A stone cottage was unoccupied while we lived on the estate, but later became the Northrop home. Another house was occupied by Mr. and Mrs. Johnson. Mr. Johnson worked in the factory. A fourth house was at the entrance to the estate and was called "the gatehouse." The style of architecture was "Hudson River Bracketed," a vernacular Gothic style that featured peaked rooflines, pierced barge-boards, arched windows, and revealed vertical construction (the kind found in movie presentations of Washington Irving's *The Legend of Sleepy Hollow*).

Several years later my father's brother and sister-in-law, by his first marriage came from Germany, and Dad saw to it that they were employed in the factory and allowed to rent the gatehouse. Uncle Peter and Anna Pyke had a daughter, Lisa, a few years younger than I. In conversations with Aunt Anna, I usually spoke German because her English was not as good as my poor German. Unfortunately, I often made mistakes speaking German and Aunt Anna thought them very funny. True my German was mixed up with English and with Pennsylvania Dutch but her criticisms hurt and so I began to use German as little as possible.

Lisa proved to be a delightful companion and we went to school together. The school was within New Hamburg, but about two miles from where we lived. Fortunately we only had to walk one mile and then we got a ride. Next to the Northrop Estate was a small prison and one of the guards had two children who were given rides to school in a prison sta-

THE BLUE JELLYBEAN…, BY KARL PRÜTER

tion wagon. The jail offered to pick up Lisa and me.
The jail assured us that we were safe with the trus-
tee driver as the reason for his imprisonment was
that he robbed a bank. He proved to be a highly safe
driver and was much appreciated on rainy and
snowy days. This was the time before school buses
so we had a two-mile walk home, which on most
days was quite pleasant. The best thing about living
on the Northrop Estate is that there were fifty-four
acres that Lisa and I got to explore. We were told
not to go near the cliff that went down to the river,
but being children we did so keeping that a secret
between us.

The school in New Hamburg was a typical
country school. I believe I was in the third grade. It
met in the same room with the fourth grade and one
teacher taught both. When she taught the fourth
grade the third graders were given assignments from
the text. The teacher and the fourth grade should
have been a great distraction, and in one sense it
was. But one couldn't help learning something from
what the fourth graders were taught. We got a lot
from the school including head lice. My mother
spotted them and immediately began to comb my
head with an angel fine comb and killed the lice by
squeezing them between her fingernails. She asked
Aunt Anna if Lisa had lice and was indignantly told
that of course she didn't. However, one evening a
louse crawled on Lisa's forehead and Aunt Anna
asked my mother for help and was given a quick
lesson on hunting lice. We found out several days
later that the school recognized they had a louse
epidemic and instructions were handed out to all the

children to take home. The instructions gave all the remedies for getting rid of the common louse.

Our days on the Estate were shortened by the Depression. Orders for carbon brushes declined and Dad's paycheck grew smaller. Mother suggested Dad should approach her old employer, Maurice Rosen, and ask him for a job. It was the right move at the right time for Maurice Rosen was a half owner of the Windsor Hotel and they needed a handyman.

Dad was glad to be employed because these were Depression years and jobs were hard to find. He was paid a living wage, but he soon discovered ways to augment his salary. We lived on LaGrange Street where my folks had purchased a two-story house. Dad quickly converted the house so that we had an apartment on the second floor that we rented out. He also discovered at the end of the street three small Jewish cemeteries and he very quickly got one of the cemetery associations to pay him for maintaining their cemetery. It became a family project, with the three of us mowing grass, clipping hedges, and planting flowers. We soon found individual families that wanted more care for their family burial plots then the cemetery provided. Mother was a flower expert and we soon were caring for many family plots. Further, word got around and the other two cemetery associations also hired us.

Mother did house work for many prominent Poughkeepsie families. Two of the families were judges and provided an extra benefit for me. Judges are expected to buy tickets to the local orchestra and to many church suppers. Buying the tickets was easy for them but they couldn't attend all the functions they were expected to support, so they often gave the tickets to mother and she passed them along to me. I became a regular concertgoer and one of the few white boys to attend chicken dinners at the black churches.

Living on LaGrange Avenue was a great place to grow up. I had the usual chores and Dad was a caring father. I helped dig a new cesspool, carried out ashes, and mowed the lawn. I remember one day trying to recall what Dad asked me to do before he left work and I decided it was to mow the lawn. When Dad got home he didn't thank me, he bawled me out because I was supposed to take out the ashes from the cellar. I remember the scolding because it is what we do with God. We do good works very often, but God has other plans for us that we neglect.

On LaGrange Avenue is where I learned even a kid could earn money. I collected rags, newspapers and tinfoil, all which I sold to the junkman. He came by every few weeks. He had a horse-drawn wagon and would shout loudly, "Rags," and when I heard him I would run out and hail him and we would negotiate over my rags, papers, and foil. One time he said he had to see what I had before he could make me an offer. So we dragged out the bundles of paper, bags of rags, and the small amount of tin foil I had collected. At his wagon he offered me what I thought was too little and I refused his offer and he refused to make a better offer. I must have been about twelve years of age but I told him since I had helped him get the stuff out he needed to help me get it back in the garage. And so we did. My mother watched all of this from the window and was amazed, amused and proud that her boy could get a grown man to drag the stuff back to the garage. I heard her tell her friends about it many times.

That was a sideline. My real work was a paper route that I had. The only investment was a basket for my bike and I had customers in the surrounding three blocks. All of the money I made went into a savings account that my mother insisted I should have, and it paid three percent interest.

LaGrange Avenue where we lived was only two blocks long and ended at the cemetery that we were maintaining. Consequently there were few boys to play with. There weren't any girls and at ten or eleven years of age. I didn't care. Everyone on the street seemed to have the same values and the same ideas about raising children. Across the street from my house and a few houses down there was a small mom and pop store run by the O'Shannies. The family was Italian (I never asked them how they got their Irish sounding name). One day a delivery truck came down the street and the O'Shannie youngster had hitched a ride on the back. Unfortunately for him, his father was standing outside of the store and saw what his son was doing. The boy got off in front of the store and his father immediately called him. As he was coming to him Mr. O'Shannie looked down the street and noticed that a number of the neighbors were observing them. In those days it meant that Mr. O'Shannie would be expected to punish the boy. He did. Then and there his son got his swats. Today, I imagine, a father wouldn't want to be observed hitting his child lest he be accused of child abuse.

Yes, we had a lot of Victorian values. I remember when a boy walking down the street with a cigarette in his mouth was stopped by a neighbor, who took the cigarette out of the boy's mouth and stamped it out on the sidewalk. The lad protested and said he would tell his dad and the man replied, "You do that kid, and I know what your dad will do to you." Parents felt free to discipline the children of their neighbors in those days.

Yes, indeed and it was time for the Pruters to make a change as well. Dad was offered a job by Mr. King, Morris Rosen's partner. He wanted Dad to become the janitor in a new apartment house he had created from an old hotel that he and Mr. Rosen owned. When he had this idea Rosen felt it was too much of a risk and King bought him out. The hotel was The Cussak House and it had been losing money. King had an altruistic motive. First, it would provide work for many unemployed and secondly it would be run as a low cost housing project. He would charge thirty dollars a month for a three-room apartment, which was ten dollars a room. There were to be a few four-room apartments that would rent for forty dollars. As a jobs project he was a bit disappointed. He offered the going rate to the workers but many of the unemployed people he contacted turned down the jobs preferring to rely on local charities.

But in due time the old Cussak House had become a fifty-apartment house and my Dad became the superintendent. Both my Dad and my mother preferred that title to janitor. It was by no means an easy job. Besides halls to be cleaned, elevator operators to supervise, Dad repaired whatever needed repairing—refrigerators, faucets, toilets, and eventually, even the elevator. On a cold winter day he would shovel in two tons of coal into the furnace. On an average day, just one ton.

We were most comfortable in our four-room basement apartment. We lived well in many respects. Mother worked at house cleaning for a number of people. I resumed delivering papers, with more success than I had on LaGrange. I took a paper route for the *Poughkeepsie Evening Star* and I discovered that I could wholesale a whole line of foreign language newspapers. I bought them from a New York City distributor and sold them to a local cigar store and newsstand. They included the *Italiano Progresso*, *Forwarts* (a Yiddish paper), *Novy Swat* (Polish), *Staatszeitung* (German), *Amsterdam News* (Black), *Daily Worker* (Communist), *Hobo News*, and a Czech paper. Many of these I sold direct to customers on my growing paper route. As the route grew I had to take Dad as a partner as it required a car to service the expanding route. One nice thing is that gas could be bought for either five or six gallons a dollar.

I had plenty of money and I think I used it well. I became a YMCA member and I went to the YMCA summer camp. The "Y" membership bought me swimming lessons. I was slow in learning swimming and my inability to swim was an embarrassment for me. The "Y" also provided a place where I could play chess, shoot billiards, play pool, play Ping Pong, and read such magazines as *The Literary Digest*, *Time*, *Newsweek*, and *National Geographic*.

Going to the YMCA camp was the highlight of the year. My dad offered to match me dollar for dollar to pay for the camp. The first year I went it was for two weeks, but after than I went for three weeks every year. The camp offered everything a boy would want—swimming, hiking, canoeing, boating, fishing, bow-and-arrow target practice, canoe trips on the Housatonic River, and every kind of handicraft one can imagine.

What I wanted to do was to fish and to canoe. I went swimming because if one is going to canoe he had better be proficient in swimming.

The camp director and staff regarded me with jaundiced eyes. They tried to interest me in handicrafts, in baseball, in horseback riding, and in hiking. I rejected everything but fishing and canoeing. I was eager for the overnight trip on the Housatonic River. When we had races I managed to take all the first place ribbons in canoeing, but in swimming I never once received a first class ribbon. I did get a number of second place ribbons and that reassured me that I proficient enough to make my interest in canoeing safe.

One day I was canoeing on the lake in a canoe that was regarded as easy to capsize. Its reputation was well earned and as I leisurely paddled along the canoe seemed to have a life of its own and capsized. I was spotted and a boat was sent out to haul me in. The director was displeased and asked me why I did such a thing. I tried to explain it was accidental but my reputation as a canoeing expert did me in. The director refused to believe that it was an accident and said I was just kidding around. He suspended my canoeing privileges for three days. I was very hurt since canoeing was almost my sole purpose in coming to the camp. I am not sure that I learned anything from this experience except that people don't always believe you when you are telling the truth.

When it was time for me to go to Poughkeepsie High School, I elected to take a general business program. College was not something I gave any thought to. However, my parents constantly told me that they expected me to finish high school. Some of my acquaintances talked about dropping out but I knew it was not an option in my family. One of the things that being raised in a household where everything was supposed to be in order and a child was expected to obey is that there never was any inward struggle about such questions such as, "Should I or should I not finish high school." In the household I grew up in it was not an option, hence not a worry.

CHAPTER THREE
†
SCHOOL STRIKE AND
THE OXFORD MOVEMENT

"I now had a different Commander-in-Chief who did not approve of killing."

In my third year in school everything turned topsy-turvy. The assistant principal, whose office I was frequently called to was dismissed. Reasons were unknown and consequently there was a great deal of speculation and many rumors. He was well liked by the students and I had my own reasons for liking him. My favorite uncle, Maurice Rehling, had been a union leader and since I admired him, I was fascinated with unions and felt strongly pro-union. It was only natural that I would think our high school needed a student union and the assistant principal's dismissal seemed like a cause for a strike. I began to agitate and I managed to get a small group of my friends to join my little union. We elected Joe Buchanan president and called for a strike.

Somehow the word got out and someone informed the New York City newspapers, so that on the day of the strike there were, at least, a dozen re-

31

porters at the high school. When the students saw that they might get their pictures in the newspapers the idea of a strike appealed to many students as a real fun outing. The school bell rang and most of the students ignored it and after many pictures were taken we headed down town and marched through the Main Street business district. Out of the 1,800 students the newspapers reported that over 1,400 joined the strike. I was given an opportunity to state our case before the school board but, of course, they were not inclined to reverse themselves because of a student protest. My parents were supportive only because they saw this as a matter of strong conviction on my part. However, my mother did say to me, "When it is over don't you be the last one to go back in school." I promised, but things didn't work out quite that way and when it was over the local newspaper did note that "Pruter was the last one to reenter the school." I had no good explanation for that.

Before the strike ended, I had a life changing experience. One afternoon our doorbell rang and my father greeted Dr. James Stringham. He told Dad that he was reading about the strike and wondered if he would be permitted to talk with me. He was a Presbyterian medical missionary on leave from China and he was visiting his parents in nearby Fishkill, New York. My dad invited him in and introduced to me and then left us alone. Dr. Stringham, who asked to be called Jim, said he wanted to share some things about his life. He told me he was a missionary but said he wasn't always a good Christian. But he met a group of people that try to live their lives based on absolute honesty, absolute unselfishness, absolute purity, and absolute love. He said they called themselves the Oxford Group, that they weren't an organization but a group made up of people who belonged to many different churches. He said that meeting with the group had changed him and one of first things he did after meeting them was to go to a department store where he had to return an umbrella that he had stolen. He said it was a hard thing to do and the department store manager was surprised. But he added, if we believe it is God's will that we live lives of absolute honesty we must be honest in the future and make restitution for our mistakes of the past. Believe me, I was one puzzled teenager. I couldn't figure our why an adult would come to me and confess that he had stolen something.

Eventually I learned that the Oxford Group was a movement started by Frank N. Buchman (1878-1961), an American Lutheran minister. In 1921, he established an international fellowship, called the First Century Christian Fellowship, to share his religious views. The group attracted many students from Cambridge and Oxford, and popularly became known as the Oxford Group. Buchman taught that God could "became real to anyone who was willing to believe in Him," and that guidance could come directly from God during meditative moments. This is a type of Christian mysticism. In 1938 Rev. Buchman saw another world war approaching, and recast his movement into Moral Re-Armament, which called for moral and spiritual re-armament. He argued that if the leaders of the world could find God, world war could be averted. The Oxford Group made it a practice to recruit students whom they regarded as leaders, and my leadership in the student strike caught their attention, hence the visit from Dr. Stringham.

Before Dr. Stringham left he talked with my father and mother and told them about himself and that the group he was identified with was going to hold a camp in Pennsylvania in July and he would like to take me with him. It would have swimming baseball, canoeing, singing, and praying. However, it seemed like it would be nice, and Dr. Stringham came across as a trustworthy person and at the end of July I was off to Pocono Pines, Pennsylvania. The camp was rented from the Lutheran Church and was called Lutherland. There was a great deal of recreation, but mostly we met in a prayer meeting similar to a Quaker meeting that the Oxford Group called a "Quiet Time."

We were told that prayer was a two-way street and if we had something to say to God, He had something to say to us. We were urged to write down in a notebook the answers that God gave us to our prayers. We were told that by doing so, the answers would seem more real and we would not forget them easily. Thus everyone at an Oxford Group meeting had a little black book to write down thoughts they had, ones that were inspired by God. After an initial period of quiet we were then asked if we wanted to share the results of our prayer. That period involved in many cases people sharing their sins and the restitution they made for their sins. They labeled this witnessing. I learned that in Poughkeepsie, where I lived, there was a regular meeting of the Oxford Group, and Dr. Stringham offered to take me there if I was interested.

The most exciting thing about the Oxford Group was that they not only professed absolute love, but also as in the Bible felt that loving one's enemies was absolutely necessary. Hence they felt a Christian could not participate in war. Other Christians I had known—included members of the Lutheran Church to which I belonged—did not accept this Biblical teaching. I felt this was a hypocritical position of other Christians, and therefore knew I would leave the church when I left home. Now, however, I could stay with the Lutheran Church and give witness to Jesus' teaching about love. I returned home with a batch of literature and I was going to help change the world by telling everyone I knew about two-way prayer, and the four absolutes of "honesty, unselfishness, purity, and love." I had a little black book in which I recorded the results of my prayers, and believe me I was on fire for God.

I was intrigued by the idea that God spoke to us, and that when we asked for direction He gave it to us. I was about to begin a new life and I needed only to ask God how to begin. After much prayer and a long quiet time, I felt I knew how to start. First, I went to visit the school principal and apologized for my role in the strike. I also brought two books I had taken from the school library. I still remember the titles, *Oil for the Lamps of China* and *Merchants of Death*; the latter had the thesis that wars were caused in part by the arms dealers. It seemed credible when I read it, but after my experience in Lutherland I realized that because we did not love one another we ended up fighting with one another. After my talk with the principal I went to see the school superintendent. His reaction at seeing me indicated he thought I wanted to start another strike or defend my position in leading the strike, which had taken place only a few weeks earlier. He did listen to me and seemed genuinely glad for and interested in my visit.

Most important I had an invitation to meet with Poughkeepsians who were identified with the Oxford Group. So one evening I went to a meeting they were having in the home of a professor at Vassar College. I learned that one does not join the Oxford Group, but is expected to identify with it by living a life guided by God and by conducting his actions according to the four absolutes. The meeting was made up of a very small group and I remember the names of most of them but not all. There was Alice Fite, in whose home the meeting was held. Her husband was a professor at Vassar College; Louise Miller, a high school teacher; Dr. Robert Morgan, a dentist; Marjorie McCracken; the wife of Vassar's president; a very gentle cleaning woman; and Dr. Stringham when he was in town. I was the newest and youngest member. Like the Quakers, everyone was called by their first name.

I regularly attended the monthly meetings. I often went with the group when they attended meetings elsewhere. One meeting was in Canaan, Connecticut, at the home of a family called Dupont. They were a nice couple but had a very undisciplined son with a foul mouth. He must have been about twelve or thirteen. One of the stories I heard about the boy was about his conduct when the Episcopal bishop came for a visit. He had been warned that he must behave and he promised to. At dinnertime, the maid brought in a pork roast and the bishop apologized and said he could not eat pork. The hostess asked the maid what else could be had. She suggested lamb chops, but no the bishop couldn't eat that, she offered chicken and no he couldn't eat that. When the next entree was offered, it was too much for the boy, and he turned to the maid and said, "Just bring the old bastard an egg."

At the end of the quiet time many of those attending would share with the group what they felt God was leading them to do. Sometimes they confessed their failures during the week and would ask the group to pray for them. This public confession was often criticized by people outside of the group. My parents were invited to attend but they did not care for this form of worship and only went to two or three meetings.

I shared my faith will many of my high school friends. At one time with the help of two Oxford Groupers from New York City I arranged for a dinner. One of the men spoke to the invited guests but the two Oxford Group representatives were not overly impressed. Afterwards I was told that I needed to cultivate "key people." In short they didn't regard my friends as leadership material. I guess none of them were, and that they came because they were followers of mine.

The next big change in my life came as the result of my prayer life. In one of my quiet times, I felt strongly that God wanted me to go to college. It seemed also that He wanted me to study journalism. I went to see the school counselor and he recommended that I go to Northeastern University in Boston. Northeastern was a cooperative school. Going there was a five-year commitment. The first year I would attend classes full time and during the last four years I would go to classes one semester and the next semester I would work on a job related to my studies. The money I earned would enable me to fund my education. When I shared this with my parents they were surprised but supportive. They said they would help as much as they could and they did. They had never envisioned my going to college but had encouraged me to finish high school. They were so determined about this that I never ever thought of disappointing them in this respect. Besides I knew I would never be permitted to drop out of high school. As far as funding college I learned from the Oxford Group that if God guided one to do something He would provide.

I still had ahead of me a summer for which I had made a commitment, which I now regretted. I had signed up for Citizens Military Training Camp that would train me for an army commission. It seemed like a real good deal. I would go to Plattsburg Barracks for one month for four years and then I would be eligible to become a First Lieutenant in the U.S. Army. I had signed up in April or May, but since my experience at Lutherland I did not believe in war. I thought of backing out but that did not seem the right thing to do either. I had promised to go, and go I would. I guess I thought that what every Army base needed, at least, was one pacifist. When the time came I boarded the train for the Barracks and found myself in a totally uncongenial environment. I had no trouble with the marching and the discipline, but the language used by the officers was foul. Perhaps that was a small thing, but the assumption that we would all some day be willing and ready to march out and be prepared to shoot "the enemy" was not.

Who this enemy would be would, of course, be determined by the Commander in Chief. But I now had a different "Commander in Chief" who did not approve of killing. I prayed and meditated and asked God to help me to get through the camp and find the vocation He would choose for me. I was beginning to feel that God had chosen my career, that it would not involve carrying a gun but a pen, which would be my tool to spread the word about a God who demanded we love even our enemies. And also of course that He wished us all to live lives of the four absolutes—honesty, unselfishness, purity, and love. Shortly before the end of camp I wrote to my roommate at Lutherland, Austin Barks, and asked if I could visit him for a few days. He lived in Ottawa, Canada, and he wrote back inviting me to come.

The Army prepared to put us all on a train headed for home. When the time came I took French leave and hitchhiked to Canada. I reached Austin's home safely and for the first time in a month I had someone I could sit down and pray with. After a few days I got on the road and hitch-hiked toward Fullerton, Pennsylvania, to see my uncle Maurice. The first day of hitching I reached Syracuse, New York, and stayed at a tourist home. The people who owned it were nice and they invited me to go to an evening service at their church. I think it was a church of the Christian and Missionary Alliance. Now my experience of churches was very limited. Most of my church contacts had been with Roman Catholics and with Lutherans, and one other experience with the Methodist Church. Before leaving for Plattsburg Barracks Mrs. Spielman, a tenant in the apartment house where we lived, invited me to go to an evening service at her Methodist Church. I found the experience strange, as it lacked the formality and the solemnity of the Lutheran Church. When the minister made some announcements he asked from the pulpit if anyone could tell him at what time the Thursday night supper would be held. A member of the congregation in a loud voice gave him the time. If the pastor had spit in the baptismal font I couldn't have been more upset.

Now this night in Syracuse I was to be exposed to an even more informal Protestantism. During the service the preacher asked people to come forward and profess their faith. No one responded, but in the back there was an American Indian who had wandered in. He was highly inebriated, but apparently was seen as a potential convert. Several men went back to him and urged him to go to the altar rail and be "saved." They grabbed him by the arms and began to pull him down the aisle to the altar rail. When they got him there the preacher laid hands on him and urged to accept Jesus and be saved. I heard the Indian mumble something. I guess he said he accepted Jesus and I am sure that he knew it was the only thing he could do to get them to let him go. Whatever, his motives he seemed to have brought joy to the congregation. And, it taught me never to go to a church without knowing something about it.

When I arrived at Uncle Maurice's he was relieved to see me. Even then hitchhiking wasn't too safe. We visited a few days then he drove me back to Poughkeepsie. The final year at Poughkeepsie High School went very well. The teachers apparently heard of the changes in my life and were most friendly.

CHAPTER FOUR
†
NORTHEASTERN UNIVERSITY

"I was now more interested in trying to make things happen."

After graduation I headed to Northeastern University, located on Huntington Avenue, in the Back Bay section of Boston. The school was founded in 1898 as the "Evening Institute of the Boston YMCA," and with its technical and vocational fields tended to attract a largely working class and immigrant population. By 1916, the school had added a day program of courses and had taken the name Northeastern College (six years later Northeastern University). It was not until 1935 that Northeastern added a liberal arts program. Many of its students were the first in their family to ever attend college. Some of its students were what are called non-traditional students, much older, with families, and full-time jobs on top of their schoolwork. They were also all male. The school did not go coed until the mid-1940s. The College of Engineering was the largest and was highly respected. I went into the Liberal Arts College. Our class began with 800 students and about 300 graduated. Northeastern accepted everyone but it was a tough school to stay in.

On my first day of college, I insisted on going alone. Some girl told me how disgusted she was to see so many college students being brought to school to enroll. She felt they were children needing to hold mommy's hand. I was immature in a different way. I worried how others would see me enrolling with my parents. A month after college began my parents came for a visit and to assure themselves that I was all right. We made the usual Boston visits to Bunker Hill and Old Ironsides. I quickly found a Lutheran Church and was received with mixed feelings. It was a Missouri Lutheran Church and I came from the United Lutheran Church. Up until then I didn't know there were different kinds of Lutherans. But I attended there regularly while I was at Northeastern.

Northeastern's cooperative feature enabled me to work first for the *Boston Herald* as a messenger and later as a copyboy for the *Boston Globe*. I don't know that I learned a great deal about journalism, but I did earn money to continue my education. I had part time jobs in many kinds work—kitchen help, laundry employee, and finally a "doorman." Through the National Youth Administration (NYA) program I did janitorial work at the college for fifty cents an hour. Initially, the NYA required you to fill out a mountain of paper work every ten weeks to continue on the job, but after the war began all you had to do was to show up in their office and you were hired.

A friend of mine, Paul Hogue, got me a job at the Sanitary Kitchen. It was a restaurant run by three Christian Scientist old ladies. My job was to take the food trays for the orders that had called down to the basement kitchen and place them on a dumb waiter and send them upstairs to the waiters. Nothing was ever touched by hand, befitting the name of the restaurant. We used tongs for everything. The owners were good to the male help but hard and unfair to the female help. The latter were mostly young Irish girls who came in early in the morning and scrubbed the floors on hands and knees. One time I heard one of the owners get after one of the girls to move some heavy milk cases with these exact words, "Grace, move those milk cases otherwise the boys will have to do it."

My favorite job was in the House of Cleanliness. It was a laundry depot run by a bookkeeper. Another student and I shared the job and we took turns being manager. If someone came in with a complaint we took our turns handling it. We didn't have many complaints since our loss and damage rate was low compared to other similar places. In those days Arrow shirts were expensive, being priced at $2.00. Whenever a shirt was lost it was always an Arrow. We made good by giving the customer a certificate for two dollars. Occasionally a customer complained that it didn't seem fair since it meant he had to risk having us wash and iron another one of his good Arrow shirts. We didn't have too many complaints except for one customer whose bundle almost always had an item missing or damaged. We tried to make a joke out of it and even went as far as to play a practical joke. He was a young bachelor living with is mother so one day we gathered together some female garments which had gotten separated from their owners and put them in his bundle knowing his mother always opened the bundle. He took the joke in a friendly spirit.

Our biggest problem was not with the customers, but with the owner. As he was a bookkeeper he should have known better, but he was forever coming in and taking money from the cash register. That would mean the laundry wasn't paid on time and would threaten from time to time not to send our laundry. For me it was a good lesson. I learned that when you have a business you make certain all of the receipts stay with the business until it is time take the profits.

My last part time job, doorman, enabled me to devote a lot of time to study. I had the job in my last semester and finally made the Dean's List. I worked for the Croyden, which was an upper class apartment house. My boss, Don Lancaster, explained to me that my job was to sit behind a desk in a small office. I could do my studies, read or twiddle my thumbs. My responsibility was to watch who came in. I was to keep out the undesirables, and occasionally be asked to do some small things for the tenants. There weren't many. One that I recall was an occasional call from a Navy captain who managed while repairing things like his wife's iron to blow fuses. He would call on the phone and ask me to change the fuse for him. I was glad to be of service to him, especially since he would tip me two dollars for performing this "mighty" task.

My first two weeks on the job were very disturbing. I never had a job where I did virtually nothing. But I was paid twelve dollars a week, and since I had nothing to do I was certain the job would end.

This uneasy feeling ended when at the end of the second week Don Lancaster handed me my check and said because I was handling the job so well that beginning with my next week I was getting a two-dollar a week raise. I never imagined that one could get a raise for doing nothing well.

Since I was a journalism student I joined the staff of the school newspaper, the *Northeastern News*. I was on the Northeastern paper some time before I was promoted to feature editor. Among the students on the paper was Nat Hentoff, who years later developed considerable fame as a jazz critic and a civil libertarian. Nat and I each took a stab at writing a humor column, but in truth we each only had one column or two of humor in us before the well quickly ran dry.

I did one feature on the universal language Esperanto. I took advantage of free classes in Esperanto sponsored by a Bahai group. I also wrote a short article on the status of Esperanto in Europe, which I submitted to the *Modern Language Journal*. They published it in their February 1943 issue and I received an A in my creative writing class. The professor had said he would give an A to any student in the class who got something published. It was my first published article outside of the Northeastern paper. I received two free copies of the *Journal* for my effort. I also wrote an article for the Northeastern paper entitled, "America Must Help German Recovery." I think the FBI picked up on that in its investigation for my application of conscientious objector status. The FBI also discovered I had read *Mein Kampf.* They found that because I returned it to the library when it was overdue. The Dean pointed out to the FBI agent that we were supposed to read *Mein Kampf* and *Das Capital* as part of our studies.

The college chapel was only being used one day a week. Various clergymen were invited to conduct a service and give a sermon. Dean Charles Havice who was in charge of the chapel tried to bring in preachers with a reputation. They were well known but usually did not meet the needs of the students who attended. What the students told me what was missing, was that the guest preachers almost never said anything about what faith meant to them personally. I managed to get one Lutheran pastor from Cambridge to come and he went well with the students. He had no great reputation and looked like a day laborer but he was down to earth and had appeal to the students at Northeastern. After speaking with a few students we decided to ask Dean Havice if we could meet in the chapel four days a week and hold a service of our own. Permission was granted but the Dean told me some time later that it was with a bit of apprehension. He wasn't sure what kind of group he was giving permission to and at that time Northeastern was just growing and very fearful of any unfavorable press.

What he didn't want were some extreme fundamentalists. Well we were far from that. I think, however, that we could be classified as a highly eclectic group. One member of our group was my journalism colleague, Nat Hentoff. We ran the meeting pretty much patterned after an Oxford Group meeting. It was silent except for contributions each member made by offering something he had read that struck him as worth thinking about. They

48

ranged from Bible selections to selections from Clarence Day's *Life with Father*. I think Nat suggested the Day book. We read some material from the classic Catholic tradition, and some was "pop" religion that was fashionable in the '40s—that is, Norman Vincent Peale and Harry Emerson Fosdick. But we were a group of twenty or thirty young men striving to find God and to change the world.

I must confess that I neglected my studies by giving more time to Oxford Group meetings and Lutheran Church meetings than I should have. God certainly did not direct me in all the "religious" activity. I was a disappointment to a scholarship group from Vassar College, which had been giving me something like $15 a month since I entered Northeastern. First because my marks were not what they should have been nor could have been. Secondly, when the news reached them that I had chosen to register as a conscientious objector they withdrew the scholarship. God certainly was watching over me for I was easily able to find work that enabled me to meet all my expenses.

The war had a powerful effect on me. I had turned to God when I discovered a small number of people who took Christ's Words literally and renounced war. The Oxford Group did not take a strong stand but created a movement, which they called Moral Re-Armament, which attempted to lead men to peace without meeting the issue head on. At the same time I was being led to the Church. Christ had given us His Church and I needed to be part of it. I saw I was making the Oxford Group my "church" as were so many of those identified with the Group. I also realized I would not be happy as a newspaper reporter. I was more interested in trying to make things happen that writing about what was happening. I felt strongly that the Christians and Christ's Church could change the world. And I have never lost that faith.

I had also been attending Mt. Vernon Congregational Church on Sunday evenings. They had a program for college students that attracted about four hundred students from many of the nearby colleges. In addition to an evening service, the program included study groups and discussion groups. The church's program gave me a chance to learn and also to give witness. Also it was here I met my future wife, Nancy Lee Taylor.

I remember little about my introduction to Nancy, but I do recall she was carrying a copy of Kahlil Gibran's *The Prophet*. Here was a girl who was interested in the writing of a modem mystic and therefore was a girl I wanted to know better. I recall asking her after the meeting was over if she would join me at a nearby restaurant for coffee and a bite to eat. I don't think we did much eating there, but we had a long conversation and it was the beginning of a very short courtship. Nancy was a graduate of Simmons College where she had earned a Bachelors Degree in Library Science. She was working as a librarian in Whitinsville, a small community not far from Boston. She came by Boston's transit system each week to Boston to attend the college group meetings at Mt. Vernon Congregational Church. After we met she started coming to Boston on Saturday and we would get together for long walks along Boston's Esplanade or visits to the Isabella Gardener Museum.

After my graduation from college in June 1943, I was offered a job as Director of Recreational Therapy at the Metropolitan State Hospital. It was an ideal situation. I was planning to attend the Lutheran Theological Seminary at Philadelphia in the fall, but this would allow me to stay in Boston near Nancy, and also to earn money for my education at seminary. I didn't realize at the time, but the job enabled me to pick up some new skills, which I was soon going to need in Philadelphia. I enjoyed my work at Metropolitan and the people I worked with. I had two young Occupational Therapists (OTs) as assistants and ran a very varied program. My department got patients involved in bowling, baseball, roller skating, and various exercise programs. One day the director of the hospital came to me and asked if I could teach tennis and I told him that I had never played tennis. His response was that I needed to learn and the following week he expected me to have a tennis class. I asked one of the OTs, Barbara Duenweg, to join me one hour a day and we would teach one another to learn tennis, by the book. We managed to keep one lesson ahead of the patients that we were teaching.

I found the work with the mental patients stimulating and rewarding, but the state care left much to be desired. We had 1,800 patients and I estimated that only about 400 were receiving any kind of treatment. But it was highly satisfying when a patient was cured and released from the hospital. During such activities as bowling, roller-skating, baseball, and exercise I had many opportunities to talk with the patients and was told many times by people who overheard the conversations that my counsel seemed most therapeutic. What I learned was that I had much to learn and I looked forward to the fall when I would be at the Lutheran Seminary. Evenings at the hospital were spent playing bridge with some of the physicians. I made up a fourth and had to be taught the game. I think I became pretty good. However, whenever I got into a bridge game with my Nancy and friends, and I played the "wrong" card she would excuse it by saying, "Well after all you learned to play bridge in a mental hospital."

Believe me, it was a learning experience. For skating class one patient came with no shoes on and when I reported it I was told, "Be glad that that is all she doesn't have on." I was proud of our baseball nine and would recruit players largely from the alcoholics that were in for forty days. They were usually extroverts and were often interested in the game. We had a good time and played against Fernald Hospital for the Feeble Minded. I remember one game we lost because our pitcher had a great fear of Indians. When the referee turned out to be a black man my pitcher saw him as an Indian and his playing just went sour. I had a few patients with a sense of humor. I recruited one woman for the bowling class. I said I heard she bowled. And she wanted to know where I heard it from and I said, "A little bird told me," And her reply was, "Do you listen to them too?" She was smart enough to be kidding.

A certain Dr. Toll, a Russian woman, came to me and said she had picked ten patients that she wish me to give breathing exercises. She said she felt a lot of patients were ill because they didn't breathe properly. She sent me patients from the back wards; most were catatonic. One patient, in particular interested me. He was Annabal Godino, a former seaman. He just did not respond to exercise. When I wanted the group to do arm lifts, Annabal turn his arms around like a windmill. But one day when I was studying the patients' records one thing in his record stood out. The doctors he saw him made regular reports and Annabal's condition got steadily worse. The last notation I read on the doctor report was that he was unresponsive but enjoyed his cigarette. This was the last report of him doing anything. I went to the commissary and bought a pack of cigarettes and took Annabal to a fenced-in porch. I offered him a cigarette. No response. I put it in his mouth and lighted it. He smoked it. When he had finish I asked him to come with me back to the ward. He took his cigarette and flicked it at the fenced window. It didn't go through but dropped on the windowsill. Annabal then spoke and said, "Wait," retrieved the cigarette, and made certain it was disposed outside. I was excited, as this was the first word he had spoken in two years. From this time forward, Annabal continued to speak and the Occupation Therapy people managed to teach him how to make key holders. Dr. Toll was delighted and told me, "I told you breathing exercises would work." I didn't say anything about the cigarette episode because she was convinced beyond contradiction that breathing exercises work. This in spite of the fact that none of the other patients showed any improvement.

One thing I did learn well was that there were two types of people working in mental hospitals. First, there were many people who became "hardened" by their work with the patients and secondly there were those who developed a sense of humor and saw in their patient's illness something of their own nature. Many patients were eaten away with anger so you very quickly learned that anger could be very unhealthy and you learned to curb your own. Patients often spent hours feeling sorry for themselves so you learned how to deal with your own sorrows constructively. Many of our everyday negative reactions we could see magnified in people who became ill from the following attributes when multiplied—*i.e.*, envy, greed, hatred, parsimony, pride, etc.

I left my job few weeks early so that Nancy and I could be married and then find a job in Philadelphia that would support us. We had a simple wedding at the Episcopal Church in Brookline with a modest reception in the church hall. After the wedding we set out for Philadelphia by the way of Poughkeepsie. My folks had lent us their car and we planned on the way to honeymoon in the Berkshires. We traveled west and had no particular place in the Berkshires in mind.

When we came to Otis, Massachusetts, there was a beautiful lake on the side of the road with a small island about one hundred yards off shore. On the shoreline was a sign stating that there were cabins for rent and next to the sign there was a gong and a wooden mallet with which one was instructed to strike the gong if interested in renting a cabin. Nancy and I could not pass this up. We hit the gong and very quickly we saw a man in a canoe leave the island and head in our direction. When he reached the shore we saw he had a great Dane with him and he introduced himself as Herb Knight. We rented a cabin up in the hills, which was named Logwood. It had a fireplace and a kitchen with a propane cook stove. Nancy and I loved the place and didn't realize that over the years we would return and as the children came we would bring them along. Several years down the road, we would return and I would be invited to be the summer supply for the local Congregational Church.

But this first year we had to move along with Logwood as a pleasant memory. We went on to Poughkeepsie, returned the car to my parents, and took a Hudson River Day Liner to New York City where we boarded a train for Philadelphia. The city would be our home for the next two years.

CHAPTER FIVE
†
THE LUTHERAN
THEOLOGICAL SEMINARY

"They said the emphasis that I placed on two-way prayer, coupled with my lack of enthusiasm for theology, might lead me to depart from the Lutheran faith."

On my job search before our wedding, I applied and was accepted as the director of boys' work at the St. Martha Settlement House, an institution sponsored by the Episcopal Church. It was located at 8th Street and Snyder Avenue in South Philadelphia, in a pleasant neighborhood made up of three ethnic groups—Italians, Jews and Blacks. It also was a neighborhood of distinctive odors. Depending on which way the wind blew we could smell a brewery, a dump, or the Schuylkill River which was really nothing but an open sewer. St. Martha's provided us with a two-room apartment—a living room and a bedroom. Meals were served for the staff in a communal dining hall.

How did I manage to get the job of boys' worker? When I came on my job search I saw an advertisement in the Philadelphia paper saying the settlement house need a boys' worker. I came and was interview by Miss Blanche Nicola, a gentle lady in her mid-fifties. She wanted to learn about me and about any experience I had that qualified me for the job. I told what I did at the Metropolitan State Hospital and that I supervised patients in roller skating, bowling, exercising, tennis, and that we had a baseball team that played against other institutional teams. She listened and was obviously pleased. But then she asked a question to which I gave an evasive answer. She asked if I could give instruction in basketball. Before answering I recalled what my Uncle Maurice had told me about how he finessed his way into a pattern weaver job by honest but sly broad answers. So when I was asked if I could teach basketball I told Miss Nicola, "At the hospital I had to teach all the sports." And Miss Nicola answered me, "I am sure you did." She was more sure than I.

It took less time then I had planned to find a job so I returned to my folk's home and was temporarily unemployed. My dad had heard about the job on a coal truck but didn't think I would want to do it, now that I had a college education. I admitted they didn't teach me anything about hauling coal, but for fifty cents an hour I was sure I knew how to do it. Besides I needed money to prepare for the wedding and honeymoon trip that I had planned. I also needed time to study a book I had purchased on how to coach basketball. When Nancy and I got to Philadelphia we found that the city had a great transit system and I would have to use it to get to my seminary classes. It was an hour's ride on the subway and the connecting bus. I used the time studying how to coach basketball.

I did well. I liked the boys and they seemed to like me. I worked at the settlement house from five until nine, Monday through Friday, and on Saturday from nine AM until nine PM. After work I usually studied until twelve and one o'clock. It was a rough schedule since I had to be on the subway at six AM, if I was to make it to seminary in time for Matins at eight. Sometimes I fell asleep on the subway and went past my stop; then I was lucky if I made it back to the bus connection soon enough to arrive at seminary for my nine o'clock class. It didn't happen often, but the officials at the seminary put pressure on me to move nearer to the school.

We eventually made the move but it took place after a most important and exciting event in our lives. Nancy became pregnant and everything started out well. But early on in her pregnancy she was riding in a car with some friends and they got into a small accident. No one was hurt but our doctor wanted to be certain the baby would be all right. X-rays were taken and everything seemed fine. However, in the days ahead Nancy became unusually large and Dr. Talent insisted on calling on another doctor for his opinion. A second set of X-rays was ordered and revealed that Nancy was carrying not one baby but two. I was informed of this over the phone and Nancy, her mother, and several people from St. Martha's were waiting for the report from the doctor. Everyone was excited and pleased, but my mother-in-law noted that we couldn't afford two babies. I pointed out to her we couldn't afford one but neither could most anyone else.

Change was certainly in the air. Since the seminary wanted me to move closer we searched for an apartment in Mt. Airy in the Chestnut Hill area and quickly found one. I also found a job at the Fifth Street Methodist Mission in the North Liberty section of Philadelphia. Before we moved to Chestnut Hill, the twins were born, on July 1, 1944. However, we were told that one twin, whom we named Robert, had contracted infectious diarrhea and would not be released from the hospital until it was over. The older twin, Hugo (older by ten minutes) was strong and healthy and entered into our hearts at once. Soon we had a call from the head nurse at the hospital. It came about ten o'clock at night and her tone was one of great urgency and concern. She said Robert was very ill, and we should contact our doctor and have her take him out of the hospital, as it didn't look as if he could live much longer. I immediately called Dr. Talent and she hurried to the hospital and after examining the baby she bundled him in a blanket, called a cab, and rushed him to the Children's Hospital. Since Robert couldn't seem to hold a formula we bought mother's milk at forty dollars per ounce. He also needed blood transfusions, and for many months I roamed the seminary grounds like a vampire and persuaded many of my fellow seminarians to donate their blood. The armed services were also seeking blood for wounded veterans so it was hard to find people who had not already given blood. It went on for months but one day we received a call that the baby was ready to come home.

I rushed to the hospital and discovered that my child showed many signs of having battled a horrible disease. He looked shriveled like an old man. But he was alive! When I went to pay the bill the person I spoke with asked me what I did for a living. I told her I was employed as a boys' worker at two dollars an hour and I attended seminary. She thought for a minute and tore up the bill and said, "I doubt if you can pay this." I never knew how much the bill was.

When I arrived home Nancy greeted us at the door with joy, but when she looked at the baby she panicked. She said, "You have to take him back, we can't take care of him." I assured that we could and that I would help. It wasn't easy for either of us. There were eleven hours in the day when either one or both of the babies had to be fed. Nancy felt she couldn't wash Robert, but I found it easy to do. The first night he was home he cried constantly so in the morning we called the hospital and we were asked if he slept on his back or on his stomach. We had laid him on his back and we were told he only slept on his stomach as his bottom was suffering from bed-sores. Sure enough it worked and he slept well after that. The only problem we had after that was that Bobby seemed always to be smiling. Knowing his condition and his close brush with death his smile always brought tears to our eyes. We shall always be grateful to God, Dr. Talent, the courageous nurse at the hospital who blew the whistle, and my many classmates who gave blood.

We enjoyed the apartment we rented within walking distance of the school. There was a small store nearby and although some food was rationed our family had four ration books. The twins didn't eat much and Bob was on a formula called Similac. It came in a powder and smelled very bad, but it worked and the baby fast caught up with his sibling.

We couldn't get a phone but the tenant on the floor above us allowed us to use his which he put on the floor just outside his door. It proved handy and we were most appreciative of it. However, on New Year's Day it rang early and not wanting to disturb the other tenants I raced up the stairs and at one point I put all my weight on the big toe of my right foot. The pain was excruciating, but I did manage to get to the phone. When I answered my mother-in-law wished me "Happy New Year." I was laid up for a week with that toe. I suspect my boss, Mr. Levit, suspected me of malingering. He did come to see me and found that my sick leave was well deserved.

After we had spent some months in the apartment, a strange thing happened because our landlady, Joan, wanted us to move so she could get a higher rent. This is where a famous film actress Hedy Lamarr enters the story. Many people have a tendency to fantasize about places they would like to visit, jobs they would like to hold, and very frequently loves they would like to have. I never did. Probably because I found my true love when I met Nancy. However, I felt left out of the fantasy love so I decided Hedy Lamarr would be mine. I knew nothing about her. I never saw a motion picture in which she played. I never read about her or even saw her picture. But she was much talked about by people and on the radio. Anyway, I picked her. Joan lived on the first floor of her home and we lived on the second floor. Every morning I would come down to a front hall shared by both of us and look for my mail, which Joan would place on a little table. When I looked at it, if Joan was present, I would remark that there was no letter to me from Hedy Lamarr, and I would imply that Joan was withholding it. It was a fun game but it soon had unexpected consequences.

During the war years, America had price controls on everything including apartment rent. Joan was not happy about this and felt she should get more rent. But the only way she could get more rent was to have us voluntarily move out or to have us evicted for cause. We weren't about to move since I still had another year to go to seminary. She then served us with an eviction notice. We appealed the case to the Office of Price Controls (OPC), and they arranged a hearing and we and Joan went before the price control officer. He informed Joan that the only way we could be evicted was if her complaint was of a serious nature. Joan quickly replied, "They're a nuisance and they have repeatedly accused me of stealing their mail!" The hearing officer asked me if this was true and I admitted that I had accused her of stealing my letters from Hedy Lamarr. The hearing officer then turned to Joan and asked, "Is that correct?" Getting an affirmative answer he then said, "Case dismissed." Despite the OPA ruling, relations between ourselves and the landlady were not soured. Of course, I didn't accuse her again of stealing my letters from Hedy Lamarr. I never again had a fantasy lover, but Nancy did. Years later she decided she loved Alan Alda. But it never got HER into trouble!

In my second year at seminary I would occasionally serve as substitute pastor when one of the nearby churches was without their pastor. My first opportunity came one Sunday and I looked forward to it with great joy. When I arrived at the Church my only concern was doing the liturgy. I had no fear about the sermon but I knew I was weak on the liturgy. My fears on this score were justified. Most Lutheran Churches use the *Common Service Book* so it should have been simple. But first, I just never thought of leading the service, and second, this particular congregation used the liturgy of the church but rearranged the liturgy. The organist tried to explain to me how their use differed from other churches, but I just didn't understand. When the service began, everyone instantly knew I was unfamiliar with it. Nancy was seated in one of the pews and there was a couple behind her and she heard the man remark to his wife, "Where do you suppose they got this man?" Fortunately the sermon went OK.

In my third year of seminary I was assigned to All Saints Lutheran Church as student assistant pastor. There I did learn how to conduct the liturgy and much about the pastor's daily duties. I also was exposed to some poorly prepared sermons. When Pastor Warnuth prepared to leave to accept a call to another church he offered me over seventy books that he did not want to take with him. I appreciated it as I always will accept books. However, I found few that I wanted and when I looked at many of them I noted Pastor Warnuth had done a lot of underlining. From the underlining I understood why the sermons were so poor as he seldom underlined the central thought in any paragraph, although it was clear that he thought he had. There were a few books that I added to my library and I offered the rest to my landlady, Joan. She was glad to get books, but she only wanted those with blue covers. She said they looked good in the bookcase.

After Pastor Warnuth left I was asked by the Central Congregational Church to be their supply pastor. I accepted the call gladly and later when they wanted me to stay after graduation I declined because I did not feel called to that church. I had applied for Lutheran ordination, but the examining committee of the New York Synod felt I needed to wait because they were not sure of my theology. They said the emphasis that I placed upon two-way prayer coupled with my lack of enthusiasm for theology might lead me to depart from the Lutheran faith. They invited me to reapply in a few months. I did not reapply for ordination from the Lutheran Church. I felt that I could get ordained but as far of the New York Synod was concerned there would always be a cloud over my head. My ordination would come, but within a different faith.

I felt I was in limbo and began to look around for another church. I saw an ad in the *Christian Century* from a church in Green Forks, Iowa. It was a Brethren Church that had a church split and the splinter group had built an identical appearing church right next to the original church. As a symbol it made Christianity look somewhat ridiculous. However, the two churches managed to reconcile their differences and reunite. In their ad they offered $1,800 a year and parsonage.

The parsonage was very nice, but it had neither electricity nor running water.

There was a hand pump next to the sink and there were kerosene lamps throughout the building. I was a little fearful of the kerosene lamps, with small children running around and my mother-in-law was appalled because we wouldn't be able to have an electric toaster. I could have overlooked the lack of electricity, but when I returned to Poughkeepsie they sent me a call but offered only $1,500 a year salary. I replied that the salary was not acceptable because what they were saying was that they would pay $1,800 to someone with experience. I pointed out that if they thought I could do the job, I should be paid $1,800 and if they thought I couldn't then they would be calling me if I worked cheap.

At this time, a Congregational minister who had met me at Central Congregational Church told me about a church in Jackman, Maine, that was seeking a pastor. They too offered $1,500 and parsonage and I agreed to candidate for that pulpit. Nancy and I drove up to Maine, and I preached the usual trial sermon and met with the church officers and members. When we returned to Poughkeepsie we received an offer and were happy to accept it. We shipped our furniture by freight and the family drove to Jackman in a 1931 Chevrolet that we named "Jeremiah." We arrived at a place that appeared to be the end of the earth.

CHAPTER SIX
†
MAINE

"If you can't find your house because of the snow, you should consider moving to warmer climes."

Nancy was very smart. We lived in many parts of the country and encountered a variety of cultures and conditions. Nancy was always able to adapt. She was an excellent wife and mother. Her adaptive skills were surely put to the test in the forests of Maine. We were surrounded by seven million acres of forest and only a few miles from the Canadian border. The temperature in the winter began in the morning at around thirty or forty degrees below zero and by one or two in the afternoon it would reach zero. Nancy dressed the children so they could play outside and in the summer she did what she could to protect them from black flies, the scourge of northern Maine. Both of us quickly learned we were in a different cultural and religious climate.

The Moose River Congregational Church had most of the 300 English-speaking people in Jackman and neighboring Moose River. There was a small Nazarene Church, which had about fifty people who had broken away from the Congregational Church some years earlier under the leadership of a female preacher. Near the Canadian border there was an Episcopal Church with about fifteen members who were served by a priest who visited the church once a month. The majority of people in Jackman were French Canadian and they attended the Roman Catholic Church.

For me I had to learn that as a pastor of a Congregational Church in New England that the Congregational Churches once constituted the State Church. Thus everyone in the community identified with the church although they may not belong to it. For example, a resident in the community may never have joined the church, or even attended, but when he died his family wanted him buried from the church. To me it was totally illogical. I felt if someone did not want to come to church when he was living he would not expect, or want, to be buried from the church. One Sunday I made this statement in a sermon and read a poem that went as follows:

> Whenever I pass a church I stop and
>   pay a visit.
> So that when at last I am carried in,
> The Lord won't say, "Who is it?"

My sermon and poem created a most hostile stir. Since I was young and just out of seminary I decided I needed the advice of a pastor older and more experienced. The nearest Protestant pastor lived seventy miles south of me in a small town called Caratunk. Now Pastor Arthur Sargent was in his early seventies and had served the church of

Caratunk and four others that were yoked together many years. Nancy and I met Arthur and his wife almost immediately after we arrived in Maine. I felt we knew them well and I felt at ease when I told him the situation in Jackman and the firestorm that ensued when I gave my sermon suggesting that people who didn't come to church when they were living shouldn't insist on being brought there when they were dead. Arthur listened patiently and then asked me, "In giving the sermon do you think what you said was right?" I said, "I did" and I repeated, "And everyone in the town is angry over what I said." Arthur looked at me a bit puzzled and said, "If you were right, what is your problem? I don't think you have one." After a cup of coffee and a piece of cake we talked about more pleasant things.

On the drive home I said to Nancy, "When I get to be seventy, I suspect, I won't think having a whole town mad because of what I did was right seem like a problem." Nancy agreed and after we both reached seventy we no longer cared when a right action made other people angry. The only long-term effect that the incident had on both Nancy and me was to develop a sense of humor.

Maine proved a good school for that. For example, Nancy was my best critic of my sermons. After Sunday service when we arrived home and sat down for Sunday dinner Nancy would offer her critique. One Sunday she complimented me on my sermon, but said I spoke entirely too loud. I reminded her that a number of old ladies sat in the back four pews and that several of them were quite deaf. Nancy's rejoinder was, "Yes, and we know who made them deaf."

After serving in the Moose River Congregational Church for a bit more than six months, I was ordained to the Congregational ministry by the Kenebec Valley Association of Congregational Christian Churches and Ministers on June 12, 1946. It was an easy move because all of my theological beliefs as a Lutheran were mine to keep. The only thing different was that there was not a synod or committee thereof that could say "nay" to what I held to be true, with the exception of the local church of course under the polity of Congregationalism.

What was wonderful about our stay in Maine was the gorgeous scenery and the number of terrific friends that we made. And making friends was not easy to do in northern Maine. In Jackman there were two classes of people—natives of Jackman and foreigners (pronounced furriners). There was a printer in town who was definitely a furriner having lived in Jackman only forty years. Now furriners might have skills the town needed but other than some specialized trade they didn't know anything. The church trustees decided that the front hall of the parsonage needed new wallpaper. They had a problem since they didn't know who in the town could do the work. When I heard of their dilemma I came to them with what I thought was a solution. I mentioned the name of one of the residents, Arthur Percious. I was told that Mr. Percious did not know how to hang wallpaper. I protested and said I had been in his house and he had done a beautiful job of wallpapering. My comment was met with a stony silence, and I was again informed that Mr. Percious did not know how to hang wallpaper. I went home and thought about it and then light dawned on me. Of course he could not wallpaper a house. He was not born and reared in Jackman. They never did find a native in town willing and able to do the work. So they hired a native to paint the hall instead.

Jackman and adjacent Moose River were unique places to live. The total population was about eleven hundred and the vast majority were of French Canadian extraction. The principal language was French and the largest church was Roman Catholic. Most of the English-speaking people were descendents of Captain Samuel Holden who came to the area in March of 1819. When we came there in 1944 there were about five English family names. I can only recall the Holdens, the Newtons, and the Hugheys. They were typical Maine folk and talked as little as possible. My predecessor as pastor of the Moose River Congregational Church, a Rev. Nuhn, stayed only two years largely because he didn't know how to deal with the taciturn nature of the inhabitants.

There was a story about the Rev. Nuhn that was told to me more than a dozen times by people who thought him strange. The story is even more strange. One day when he was visiting people in the village he came to Mr. Hughey's home. Hughey was outside painting his canoe. The pastor came and watched the painting. Neither the Rev. Nuhn nor Mr. Hughey uttered a single word until about twenty-five minutes later. Then the Rev. Nuhn managed to overcome his shyness and put the question to Mr. Hughey, "Painting your canoe, Mr. Hughey?" Mr. Hughey thought for about a minute and not being loquacious said simply, "Yup." That

was not much of a help to the Rev. Nuhn, so he
bade, "goodbye."

Each person who told me the story did so that
I would know that the Rev. Nuhn did not know how
to carry on a conversation. Not one of them, however, thought Mr. Hughey's reply was to put it
mildly a bit short and not helpful in the art of verbal
communication. It is rightly said that one could get
along fine in New England with a vocabulary of two
words, "yup" and "nope."

In any community there are a few hustlers
and a few people who don't hustle, because they are
in a rut. Change and new were foreign concepts in
Jackman. I remember talking to our church clerk.
She was a fine and generous soul, but never entertained a new idea in her entire life. One day I went
to her with an idea that I thought might help the
church. I gave her the details and then asked her:
"What do you think of it?" Her reply was swift and
succinct. "Well, Mr. Pruter, I will have to think
about it and then weigh the pros and cons against
it." It was hard to serve in any situation where people weigh the pros and cons against every new idea.

On the other hand, there is Ruel Holden, one
of Samuel's descendants. He had built on an island
in the nearby lake a very successful summer resort.
Someone asked him one day why it was that he was
successful where so many others had failed. His reply is a classic: "Well," he said, "Before I do anything I ask every man, woman, and child in the entire village for advice, and then I do as I damn
please."

Among the friends I made in Jackman was
the Rev. Ernest Smith, pastor of the Nazarene

Church. Theologically we had nothing in common but we enjoyed hunting together. Hunting for us was more than a sport because it was during the war and we were seldom able to get meat at the stores. Once a week a truck called "The Boundary" came into town and brought what groceries could be bought and on a good week they had frankfurters. So if we could shoot four partridges each, it would be most helpful. So during partridge season we went out every day and since they were very plentiful in an hour's time we had our limit.

But we did differ on theology and Christian practice. Ernie would never buy a Sunday paper because he thought people worked on Sunday to produce it. When I told him that the Sunday paper was prepared on Saturday night, it didn't change his position because he said, "If people see me buying a Sunday paper they will think I am breaking the Sabbath."

We had many differences over theology and faith. But only one caused some strain between us. That was over the Nazarene doctrine of total sanctification. Ernest explained that the Nazarene Church was a "holiness church," and was thus made up of people who had received total sanctification. After receiving it they never again commit any sins. I had my doubts but Ernest assured me that his people were a holy people. Well he could believe it, but I would believe that we are all sinners. Surely this should cause no rift between us. Of course there was the Sunday, I preached a sermon entitled, "Generation of Vipers." I told the congregation that there was entirely too much gossip among them. And there was. I had never lived in a community where there was so much vicious gossip. Whether there was more fornication than that in other communities I am not sure, but I had heard enough so that I felt they should be concerned. Of course, this news was carried throughout the community and the Rev. Smith made a point of saying he heard about it and was very sorry we had those problems and he was glad these things did not touch his people. "You know," he said, "they are totally sanctified." How can one answer that? I didn't try. Fortunately he didn't feel we needed to be separate. We might be radically different but apparently the "sanctified" and the "unsanctified" can hunt together and have coffee together. As Christians we are one.

The rift came one day when a couple who belonged to his church came into my study. They wanted me to marry them in the Congregational Church. "Why?" I asked. "I am flattered that you want me to marry you, but why don't you want to be married in your own church by your own pastor?" They quietly said that they were supposed to be totally sanctified and that the lady was pregnant and they wished to be married before people noticed. Further they couldn't go to their pastor and tell him of their sin. My first concern was for the couple and we had a long counseling session. I agreed to marry them knowing that the Rev. Ernest Smith would regard my action as highly unethical and a betrayal of our friendship.

In time Ernest asked me why I did it and I avoided the question by saying, "They came to me and asked me to marry them. I am not the one to ask. You need to ask them." The subject was dropped and our friendship continued as before.

Nancy and I saw Ernest and his wife Amanda regularly and shared some of the trials and tribulations of living in the near wilderness that constituted Jackman. One day we got an urgent phone call from Amanda. Ernest had gone down river to do some shopping and Amanda stepped out of the house to hang laundry. As she opened the door a rat ran inside trying to escape a mink who followed the rat inside in quick pursuit. What to do as she now had two wild creatures in the house and neither were welcome. Nancy and I went quickly to see if we could help. When we arrived the rat had hidden somewhere and the mink was searching for it. We opened the door of the house and we each took a broom, a hoe, and a rake, and kept driving the mink toward the door. It took nearly three quarters of an hour to get it out. We would often get him close to the doorway only to have him slip by us and we were back to square one. As for the rat, Amanda set a trap and that night it was caught. Ernest arrived back shortly after the mink was gone and remarked that he missed the fun. Nancy and I quickly left so that Amanda could respond to that observation.

The most important time we shared was when Nancy was due to have our third child. We had made arrangements for her to have the baby at the Greenville Hospital which was at Moosehead Lake about sixty miles away. Our car was a 1931 Chevrolet and we felt it was too unreliable to make such an important trip that was so far. The trip would have been through sixty miles of uninhabited forest. The Smiths had a newer car and offered to take us when the time came that Nancy would deliver. Shortly after dark one evening Nancy felt the first labor pains and we called the Smiths and they came quickly and we headed for Moosehead Lake. The care drove beautifully, but fifteen miles into the forest the headlights went out. We had no choice but to turn around and head back. When we got back to our house I called the one and only physician in town. Unfortunately several weeks previously I had accused him of being an abortionist. He had recommended an abortion to one of my parishioners and in the 1940s it was neither legal nor acceptable to most people. True to the Hippocratic Oath the doctor came and a few hours later our daughter came into the world. Her mother looked at her and said, "She looks so ugly." I wished I had had a camera because that was no exaggeration. Yet the ugly duckling grew up to be a most beautiful woman and remains so to this day.

The twins were very much interested in their new sister. They couldn't pronounce her name, "Nancy," so she became "C." They also didn't suspect that she would soon rule the roost. From the word "go" Nancy showed her independence. When she was put on a bottle she quickly insisted on holding it herself. Getting her to eat whole food or even baby food presented a problem. She resisted spoon feeding. I don't know how we discovered it but the only cereal she would eat was bite-size shredded wheat. She could pick it up and put it in her mouth by herself. If you tried putting something in her mouth by spoon she would spit it out. For quite a time she lived on a bottle which she could hold and the bite-size shredded wheat, which the twins named "C cookies."

Having children usually means having pets. We had two—a dog named Nero and a cat called Caliban. The animals got along together and the children enjoyed playing with them. Only once did I have to interfere with their play. Nero had picked up Caliban, as he was wont to do, and the twins wanted to rescue Caliban and they took hold of her backside while Nero with her head in his mouth pulled in the opposite direction. Fortunately Nancy saw it and sent me outside to rescue the cat. The cat lived and she and Nero continued their strange friendship.

It wasn't difficult to find things to do for recreation in Jackman, but you couldn't be too demanding. Of course, the family came first. Nancy and I enjoyed our children and spent a great deal of time with them. After they were in bed we both were avid readers and sometimes listened to the radio. Television was not unheard of but it hadn't reached into the forests of Maine. We did have a movie house and every week they offered a new movie. But I don't remember ever having gone to the movies in Jackman. We had better entertainment driving out to the town dump and watching the bears. There usually were six to ten bears going through the garbage seeking delicacies which the forest didn't offer. As long as you stayed in your car at a good distance you could safely watch their antics.

On several occasions I felt I needed to think of moving from Jackman. I grew a small garden and I felt like moving when my string beans froze in July. It didn't usually freeze in July, only in the other eleven months. If this was not a sufficient hint that I should move there was an even a stronger hint from Mother Nature that I should move to a warmer climate. One night when we had visited some friends in the community there was considerable new snow. As they were driving us home we speculated on whether the snowplow may have come by and plugged the tunnel I had made from the front yard to the road. It was some concern because it was late January and there was a huge snow bank in front of the house that had been building since November. Snow didn't melt in Jackman until May. Sure enough the tunnel was plugged with snow and since the snow bank was fourteen or fifteen feet high and our hosts who were driving close to the bank could not see the house. It took us many minutes to figure out where the house was and then a few more to climb up and over the snow bank. We laughed about the experience but got the feeling that if you can't find your house because of the snow you should consider moving to warmer climes.

CHAPTER SEVEN
†
ORFORD AND ORFORDVILLE

"It was my job to tell people what Christ said and taught."

After two years in Maine the time had come to answer a call from two churches in New Hampshire. Such arrangements were called a yoked field and the two churches were located three miles apart in Orford and Orfordville. The Township of Orford like most New England townships was ten miles square. It was on the East bank of the Connecticut River. Orford was along the riverbank and Orfordville was three miles further east in the hills.

I knew nothing of the history of the town before I came but I soon learned a great deal. The minister had from the beginning served both churches. But originally he had resided in Orfordville. He would still had not the parishioners of Orford decided one year when the churches were without a minister to play what is known as "dirty pool." The two churches called a new minister who accepted and when he arrived by train was met by members of the Orford congregation and brought to a parsonage they had secretly purchased. The new minister did not know that the parsonage had always been in Orfordville. Only after he moved in bag and baggage did the people of Orfordville discover the ruse. They were outraged but had to accept the fait accompli. Until this very day the pastor of the Orford and Orfordville churches lives in Orford.

The parsonage was an impressive house. Over one hundred years old and made of brick. The boards in the attic floor are wide, obviously cut from virgin timber. The house had nine rooms, and the living room and the bedroom above were enormous. Both rooms had fireplaces, although we never used the one in the bedroom. The house had steam heat and we were able to purchase both wood and coal. The furnace was adequate but it never is able to heat all the rooms at once. We had to turn the heat in one of the smaller rooms off for a while. I called it to the attention of one of the parishioners and was told that that was impossible because the system had been designed by an engineer. Maybe so, but we were never able to heat all the rooms at one time.

Before coming to Orford we had purchased a large Lafayette. I don't know what kind of car the previous pastor had but the garage was too small for our vehicle. The Lafayette stuck out about eighteen inches and so the garage doors could not be shut. We called this to the attention of the congregation and the Ladies Society hired a carpenter and had the garage enlarged. We were truly grateful but unfortunately the Lafayette had seen better days and we had to buy a new car. It was probably not a wise thing to do but we bought a new Crosley station wagon, a small pillbox kind of car that was barely large enough for Nancy and me and our three small children. The members of the Ladies Society were quick to notice we could have gotten two Crosleys in the garage before they enlarged it.

However, that was the least of my worries. The big one was keeping both parishes contented. When I began my ministry in New Hampshire I was careful to do my pastoral calling alternately because I wanted both churches assured that their pastor gave them equal treatment. The Orford Church, usually referred to as the "street church," because it was on the main road going north and south, had an average attendance of about fifty-five, and the Orfordville church had an average of only four. Several factors contributed to the poor attendance in Orfordville. First was the fact that the former pastor seldom made calls in Orfordville. The people in Orfordville were made up of a few farmers, and many families following the sawmills. Most of them lived in tarpaper shacks and many were "shack ups" long before the word was made popular in the 1960s. The pastor gave different sermons in the Orfordville Church and the Orford Church. He explained by telling a few people that the people in Orfordville wouldn't understand the sermons he preached in Orford. Attendance at Orfordville noticeably dropped after that statement was passed around.

After hearing about this, I made certain that I preached the same sermon in both churches, even to the point of making certain all the pauses were in the same place. I carefully made certain that I alternated my parish calls. One day in Orford, the next day in Orfordville, the next day in Orford, and the next day in Orfordville, and so on. And so on until I felt certain I had everyone's confidence that I would play no favorites.

The Orford church had a unique problem. While both churches had large endowments Orford also had a small group of wealthy people, some of whom lived on what was called The Ridge in stately mansions, which when I was there were said to have been designed by Charles Bulfinch, a well know and respected early American architect. Of the seven mansions on The Ridge, however, only one was of built in the Bulfinch style and its design was attributed to a Bulfinch disciple. Some of these seven mansions were occupied by only summer residents from New York.

Both churches relied on the Sunday offerings and the endowments to pay expenses. However, from time to time The Ridge people in Orford would meet the church treasurer and ask how the church finances were. If he said money was short, they would write him a check on the spot and it took care of things until the next need came along. Of course, this was New England and the folk were very frugal. How frugal I soon learned.

The church building in Orford is extraordinarily beautiful. It is frame but nevertheless Gothic in style. It is the kind of church which if you area tourist driving by you would want to stop and go inside. Unfortunately like most Protestant churches during the week the doors were locked. I spoke to the trustees about keeping the church open but they expressed the fear that someone might come in and steal something or even vandalize the building. I thought about it and then went to see Gould Richmond, our insurance agent. I asked him what it would cost to insure the church against vandalism and mischievous damage. He looked in his rate book and said we could add it on our present policy for nine dollars a year. Armed with this information I went to the church trustees and ask them to reconsider their decision about leaving the church doors open. They agreed if I would open them every morning and close them at sundown. The deal was done.

A few days later I get a call from Mr. Richmond and he told me that he quoted the rate on the additional insurance on the assumption that we had extended coverage. He found that we only had fire insurance and that to add extended coverage would cost an additional $60.00. I gave it a few minutes thought and told him to go ahead and add the coverage and the vandalism clause. The total cost now came to $69.00. When I told my wife she asked, "What are you going to say to the trustees when they get the bill?" I had to confess I didn't know, but I knew I would be in very hot water indeed.

A week later the area was hit by a very strong hurricane and many buildings in town were damaged. The church tower suffered a bit of damage and my wife and I looked at it and did not think of what it meant. Later in the day the church treasurer came by said he had a local contractor look at the damage and he said the repairs would come to six hundred dollars. The treasurer said, "We just don't have that kind of money." "That is terrible," I replied, "but won't our insurance take care of it?" "It would," the treasurer told me, "if we had extended coverage but we never got it." At this point I was a bit uneasy but I did say that I thought we did. "No," he said, "we never had it." I then ventured to say again that I thought we did and that he should check with Mr. Richmond our insurance agent. He returned awhile later and said, "Gould says we are covered and he will have Mr. Horton the contractor take care of it. The trustees will sure be glad to hear this news."

I was sure that the trustees were glad, but nothing was ever said to me by the treasurer, Mr. Richmond, or the trustees. This was New England where you just didn't talk about certain things. If anyone ever speculated how and when we got the insurance I never heard about it.

We had in Orford a very straight talking, no nonsense individual by the name of Mrs. Allen. One day, a visitor from New Jersey asked Mrs. Allen what sort of people he would find in Orford. "Well," asked Mrs. Allen, "What are the people like back in New Jersey?" He replied with a pained look on his face, "That's the trouble. They are unfriendly, they gossip, they are really a bunch of backbiters." "Well," Mrs. Allen replied, "That is exactly the kind of people you will meet here."

Mrs. Allen's straight talk made for a very healthy community. There was the case of Mr. and Mrs. Bean who nobody could quite understand. Mr. Bean was a rough old cattle farmer. He would work out in the barns and come into the house with manure on his books, and where it dropped, it dropped. Mrs. Bean was very refined and a meticulous housekeeper. She often followed her husband around with a brush and a dustpan. One day at the women's society some of the women speculated on how in Heaven's name did Elizabeth ever happen to marry such a slob. "I can answer that," said Mrs. Allen. "I know." She was quickly asked how she knew, and her reply was simple and direct:

> I asked her. Elizabeth is his second wife. She is a nurse and she was called in to care for his first wife who died of a long, lingering, and painful cancer. She was impressed on how Mr. Bean cared for his wife and even more impressed by the love he had for her. When the first Mrs. Bean died Elizabeth knew the kind of man she wanted for a husband, and as soon as it was decent to do so she told him so.

Not everyone saw that side of Mr. Bean. Every morning he drove about a quarter of a mile to the local garage just to talk with the men that come there to chat. For some reason he always drove on the left side on a short but curvy road. One day he had a collision with one of the local residents and she got out of her car quite irate and said, "Mr. Bean you are on the wrong side of the road." An equally irate Mr. Bean gave a short and one will agree a logical answer, "Of course I was on the wrong side of the road. Everyone in this town knows that I drive on the wrong side of the road, and no one has ever hit me except you, you damn fool."

He could be a man with a quick answer. I came into the barnyard one day shortly after he had purchased a front loader. I was surprised because the yard was small and he didn't have a large herd. I remarked that it was a nice loader but did he need it was so small an operation. "Nope," he said, "but who wants to handle this muck!" Made sense.

These small New Hampshire farmers turned a handsome profit although few of them would admit it. I remember talking with one dairy farmer as he bemoaned the plight of the farmer—hard work, long hours, and very little to show for it. I stood along side his new Buick while he poured forth his list of woes. When I came into the house my wife asked me what I had been talking so long with Mr. West about. I replied. "Like every farmer in town he was telling me how bad farming is, and how they are all going broke. I wouldn't mind it so much if they just didn't tell me while they sat in their new Buicks."

I am not picking on the native New Englander for the little town had some strange men and women among the "summer folk." These people came from New York, New Jersey and all the southern New England states. There was, for example, Ola Miller and her two daughters. According to town gossip she was a "grass widow," who had been a rich man's secretary and then married him, and received a handsome settlement at the divorce.

I first met her when she came for the summer and attended Sunday church service. After the service, she told me who she was, although she assumed I knew and asked me to come and see her. I didn't realize it, but it was a summons. When I went to see her she said she was concerned about my sermon, which was directed at her. I told her I didn't understand, because I didn't know who she was. "Of course, you knew who I was and that is why you preached a sermon about rich people. You said a rich person had as much chance of getting into the

Kingdom of Heaven as a camel getting through the eye of a needle. Furthermore, you mentioned divorce and you obviously knew that am divorced." I did point out to her that I wasn't the one who made the statement regarding a rich person' s chances of getting into heaven, but Christ said it. "Yes, I know, but you repeated it." I pled guilty, and in my defense I stated that it was my job to tell people what Christ said and taught. That is why I was called to this church. Before I was able to leave, she told me that she had given the organ to the church. I merely said, "We appreciate it," and made my departure.

Having donated the organ I then realized she was one of the church's VIPs. So I went to see Mr. McCann, the church treasurer who lived nearby. I told him what had happened and he asked just one question, "When you left did she say 'Goodbye?'" I told him, "Yes," and he breathed a sigh of relief and said, "Good, then she will still continue to make payments on the organ."

I soon learned a lot more about Mrs. Miller. She and her two daughters came to the post office for the mail every morning. They rode in procession. Each had their own convertible and Ola Miller led the procession followed by her two daughters. They emerged from their cars together, picked up the mail at the post office, and then reentered their respective cars and drove home in procession.

Now Mrs. Miller as the proud owner of forty acres of bottomland wanted to care for the property as any Lord of the Manor should. While she was in New York she entered a flower shop and bought a ton of sheep's manure in fifty-pound sacks and had it shipped to her New Hampshire manor. The natives were surprised since cows and sheep dotted her every acre and made their own personal contribution to the manure pile. Further when she arrived she went into the barn and inspected the manure pile. She expected to see fifty pound sacks tightly filled with sheep manure. Now sheep manure when it dries has a tendency to shrink and what she saw where many bags of manure and they all seemed to be less than full. She accused her farm hand, Henry Bean, of stealing some of the manure. He was taken back and a little angry. Before walking off from the job he said, "Mrs. Miller, my mother brought me up right. I remember sitting on her knees and she said to me, 'Henry don't you ever steal. Especially you should never steal sheep manure.' "And I never did." He turned around and left.

Mrs. Miller's buying habits engaged the community to no end. At church fairs and other town events, she would shop and buy various wares that interested her. For example, one lady was selling jars of jams and jellies. Mrs. Miller bought a dozen of each of the varieties that took her fancy. It was then noticed that every purchase she made she always bought a dozen pieces.

Now having a mother who has money can be an advantage in many ways. For example, the second summer I lived in Orford the girls took three weeks to visit Europe. I wish every college-age child would spend three weeks in Europe. It can be very educational and enriching. When they returned from their trip they were anxious to talk about it, and I listed attentively. They started off by telling me that during their three weeks in Europe they visited seventeen countries. On hearing this, my heart sank. They had learned all about how railroad stations looked in many different countries but learned nothing about the people or their culture. I wondered how often we send our children into the world poorly prepared to understand and appreciate what they see?

In many ways the most remarkable man in Orford was Guy Huntington. When I came to candidate for the church, the former pastor's wife introduced us to Guy. She pointed out that he collected the ashes from the parsonage. She said nothing further but she had much to tell us about the seven families who lived on The Ridge. He collected their ashes and the ashes of almost everyone else in town. He and a small crew of helpers mowed the lawns of the families on The Ridge. Huntington was also the Railway Express man, the town marshal, the church janitor, and he regularly sponsored movies and other shows at the town hall. But I remember and appreciate most of all what he did for a nephew and his wife. Both were developmentally disabled, but with Guy's mentoring the nephew learned to drive a truck and worked regularly. The couple was always neatly dressed and maintained a clean and orderly house. The couple was able to live independently and was a credit to the community and to Guy Huntington. He may have been the man who collected the ashes at the parsonage, but he was also easily the most important man in town.

A resident by the name of Dr. Hall, who moved into Orford from the Boston area, also got the town talking. He had been practicing medicine in a very wealthy suburb. Once settled in Orford, however, he came to the conclusion that many of his patients didn't want to get well. They did as a New England expression went, "They were enjoying poor health." In any event he bought a small dairy farm. When the natives found out that he had never farmed before they wondered how he expected to make it. Someone asked him how he hoped to succeed when he had never engaged in animal husbandry. When he told them he had a good book on animal husbandry he was the butt of local humor for some time. That is until two years later he won a state award for having the best dairy farm in the state. His success was do to select breeding through artificial insemination, something which at that time few New Hampshire dairymen practiced.

Dr. Hall had a wife and two boys and their life revolved around the farm. When it was proposed that the town build a center for young people Dr. Hall was opposed. The idea of the center was to offer activities to keep the young people out of trouble. Dr. Hall felt the center would take young people out of the family circle. His children he felt had sufficient work and recreation within the family circle and that is what he wished to preserve.

On the lighter side one nice couple in the town had a big problem with Sears. Like many of us living in the country they bought from "The Book," as the store's mail order catalogue was commonly called. One day they bought a pair of trousers and in due time it arrived. Shortly after it arrived a second pair was delivered. So the lady of the household returned the second pair. In response Sears sent them another pair. She returned this one also with a letter stating they were very satisfied with the first pair. It still didn't work but went on for still another pair.

Finally, she came to me as her pastor and asked whether it would be "right" to keep the latest arrival from Sears. I told her that she had done her best to straighten the matter out and I thought it would be alright if she regarded the latest contribution from Sears as one of their charitable gifts.

Pastors who served in the late 1940s and early 1950s encountered an unusual problem dealing with the war that was over. First they were asked to conduct a memorial service for the soldiers who were killed. Although they were buried overseas those who attended the services for them felt comforted and they felt closure. But almost a decade later they were notified that the bodies of their loved ones were being returned and the effect was to open wounds that had long since been healed. I was asked to offer a memorial service when the bodies were returned and they were difficult and heart wrenching. We tried the best we could to offer a service that would once again help heal the trauma of a loved one's loss. I assure you it was harder than the first memorial service. When the decision was made in Congress to bring the bodies home, I am sure no one asked the advice of the clergy. This is one of those decisions on behalf of a group represented by lobbyists that frequently slip through Congress. New Englanders, on a whole, were a strong and stoic people. There are fewer tears at a New England funeral than anyplace in the country where I have served as a pastor. But there was not any less caring or any less feeling of loss.

There are a few problems in many New England towns due to the fact that non-church people and their families felt they had a right to be buried in the town church. Often some of them would be members of some lodge and want the lodge to participate in the service. I tried to handle this by saying that after the Christian rites were offered I would step aside and the lodge could do its thing. Once in Orford I was informed that I didn't need to go to the cemetery as the lodge would take care of the committal at the grave site. I quickly informed the lodge that they were welcome to have any service they wanted but since I had been asked to offer the Christian rite of the church, I would do so and see the body all the way to the grave. And so I did. Fortunately everyone seem satisfied.

I wriggled out of that one, but I had to face the fact that not everyone was pleased with my ministry. As I pointed out during my Maine experience, New Englanders were people of few words. But they expected you not to be like them. Admittedly when I would walk about town my mind wandered in many directions. I might be thinking about my next sermon or the next article I would write. On a few occasions I may have failed to greet some one I met along the way. One of these was Phyllis Lawrence who lived in one of the houses on The Ridge. At a Ladies Society meeting she made the statement that the new pastor (yours truly) was not, at all friendly. Mrs. Allan, a very outspoken New Englander responded in my defense. She said, "Your trouble Phyllis is that you want a bottom pincher and we have had several of those and we don't want another one." As far as I know Mrs. Lawrence never again complained about me, at least not at the Ladies Society.

CHAPTER EIGHT
†
In and Around the
Connecticut Valley

"But Judge, that was in Vermont!"

Orford was not the only city in the Connecticut Valley with colorful people and stories. One of the most beloved persons was Fred Dixon who was pastor of the church in Piermont the town just north of us. He had been a missionary in Africa and sought a quiet existence in Piermont. Fred Dixon's African experience was not a great help in Piermont. One day he visited a woman and she told him of the terrible pain she was having in her knee. Fred did what he had done many times in Africa. He offered prayer with both hands on the lady's knees. The story the lady told implied that Piermont had some kind of sex fiend as their pastor. Fred and his wife came to our house and were very visibly upset by the lady's accusations. Well, he couldn't have been too upset as he referred to the lady as "that old bat," which for Fred was strong language. Shortly afterwards they decided it was time to retire and they went to Henicker, New Hampshire, seeking a quiet life in a house they purchased that had adequate space for a rose garden. Unfortunately not long after they arrived Fred suffered from a heart attack. I shall never forget the note that he wrote to me. It went like this. "I am praying that God will give me enough strength to tend to my roses or enough patience to leave them alone." No one could have said it better.

One of the nicest persons I met while in the Upper Connecticut Valley was Ralph McGinnis. He lived in Fairlee. He had been head of a large school of art in New Jersey and was living a quiet life in Fairlee and doing some painting. While visiting him on one very cold day in the middle of winter he said a neighbor had just come by and invited him to go with him for a drive on the thoroughly frozen Lake Fairlee. It was apparently a local sport. You got into you car and brought your speed up to sixty and then hit the brakes and the car would spin around and around. It sounds like great fun but Ralph declined the offer for the ride.

Living in New Hampshire on one side of the Connecticut River and Vermont on the other was an experience. The Vermonters and the New Hampshirites had strong feelings about one another. I learned this very quickly when I visited one of my new parishioners who lived on the riverbank. His view of Vermont was not the best. The Fairlee town dump was directly across the river from him. But he told me that he always took his trash to that dump. I asked why since we had a dump in Orford that was a short distance away and he didn't have to look at it. He said, "I know but I just can't bring myself to dump my trash in New Hampshire."

Another example of this feeling came from the town drunk in Haverhill, a lovely town a few miles north of Orford. They had a town drunk who was always getting picked up for public drunkenness and usually spent a night in jail every time he was arrested. But the judge one day warned him that the next time he was drunk he would have to serve thirty days in jail. Of course there was a next time and the judge was exasperated. He pointed out to the miscreant that not only did he get drunk the night before, but two weeks earlier he was arrested for drunkenness in White River. "But judge," he protested, "that was in Vermont!"

When we came to Orford the Fairlee Church was without a pastor. They began to search for a suitable candidate and they had several men and women come to candidate for the position. That meant they would come and conduct the Sunday service and be interviewed by the congregation. What the congregation was mainly interested in was the future pastor's preaching ability. Of course, every minister has, at least, one good sermon that he could offer. The first candidate they heard was of Japanese descent and the talk I heard afterwards that they did not want him because of his race. One Fairlee resident told me this, and I responded, "You are not calling him for breeding purposes. All you should be concerned about is he the right man for the job." I found out about the next candidate the next Sunday morning, when four Fairlee ladies came to the Orford Church for the morning service. After the service they told me that the Fairlee Church had a woman candidate for the service. I think that was the only time anyone from Fairlee attended the Orford Church.

The next candidate was the Rev. Ralph Kraut, who was serving a church in Lunenburg, Massachusetts. Ralph and his wife, Gertrude, were destined to become close friends to Nancy and me. Ralph proved to be the successful candidate and after the service and the interview with the congregation, the trustees met with Ralph and indicated that they felt the congregation would offer him $2,400 annual salary and pay their moving expenses from Lunnenburg. After the meeting the Krauts drove back to Lunenburg with high expectations. They liked the church and the people seemed very nice. But when the call came in the mail a few days later they learned that the congregation accepted the trustees recommendation for the $2,400 annual salary but made no mention regarding moving expenses. That should have told the Krauts something about how they would be treated by the Fairlee congregation. But they were among God's most naive children.

When they began their ministry things seemed to go along pretty well. When the annual vacation came in August the church obtained a young minister to be the supply pastor. The young man was full of vitality and organized the young people for a class in square dancing. When the Krauts returned they found a congregation talking about how wonderful the supply pastor was. The board of deacons approached Ralph and suggested that he conduct square dancing classes. Now Ralph had a physical disability. From birth one of his legs was shorter than the other. In addition Ralph's talent, and he had much, did not lie in square dancing or even in conducting youth activities.

One day when I came out of the Fairlee grocery store one of Ralph's parishioners stopped me and indicated she wished to speak with me. She had high praise for Gertrude, and several times told me how intelligent she was. Now Gertrude was a very fine lady, but intelligent she was not. When I returned home I told Nancy, "Ralph is in trouble." She asked me what made me think so. I explained that in any parish if the congregation is unhappy with the minister's wife their dissatisfaction would be expressed by talking about what a wonderful person their minister is. Left unsaid was, "Too bad he has a shrew for a wife." If they are they are unhappy with their pastor, they talk about how wonderful his wife is. And when they praise her for attributes that she doesn't possess he is really in trouble. The gossip went on for some time and only died down when Ralph asked for a leave of absence. He heard from his brother that medical experts have found a way of correcting his physical disorder. He investigated at the hospital at Hanover, which was connected with Dartmouth College, and the doctors upon examining him assured him that they could lengthen the short leg. They said the operation was easy but the muscles of the leg had atrophied to some extent and after the operation he would require six months of physical therapy. The brother was able to finance the operation and support Ralph and his family for at least a year. Ralph asked the trustees of the church to grant him six months leave and then let him be the supply preacher for another six months. As supply preacher he would receive the princely sum of fifteen dollars a week. After that he would return as their full-time pastor.

Before he had the operation done, Ralph and Gertrude visited us and told us what they were about to do. When he had finished telling me the details, I asked him, "Ralph, what are they going to pay you when you return?" He looked surprised and said, "Why what they always paid me $2,400 a year. Why do you ask?" I told him that he should have clarified this because I did not trust the "lemon heads," which was my frequently used term for his parishioners. I probably should have refrained from my derogatory aspersion, especially since it upset Gertrude whenever I used it. Despite what I said, Ralph and Gertrude felt there was no problem and were confident that the operation would be a success and that the trustees would do the right thing by them.

Eighteen months went by and Ralph and Gertrude came to see us. When they came into the house it was obvious that something was wrong. Unfortunately my worse fears were realized. The Fairlee Church was glad to have Ralph back as their full-time pastor, but felt they could only afford to pay him $2,000 a year. Gertrude asked, "How did you know this would happen? Did you talk with anyone in Fairlee?" "Gertrude," I said, "No I didn't talk with anyone, but knowing the lemon heads, I felt this is what you could expect." It was said, and true, that the Fairlee Church had not lost any membership and their income had not dropped, but they took advantage of their pastor.

There were good people in Fairlee but, for some reason not many of them seemed to get on the church boards. On the lighter side, the gossip was that the choir had a Sunday morning pool. All the choir members put up a quarter and gave their guess on how long the pastoral prayer would last. The person whose guess was closest won the pot.

Fairlee, I must admit did have a good choir and their organist was highly competent. Orfordville, my hill parish, had a fine organ but no organist. Since services at the Orfordville church were at nine AM, we offered the job to the Fairlee organist. She accepted but she didn't have a car so I offered to drive her to the church and back. She was competent, pleased, and seemed quite proper.

One day when we were visiting with Ralph and Gertrude they mentioned that people were concerned because the church was not growing. We all agreed that in a small town like Fairlee there was little opportunity for growth. We began to talk about Fairlee residents who might respond to an invitation to become members of the church. I mentioned one of the men in the choir who seemed devout and from what I had heard was regular in his attendance. Gertrude responded, "Yes, he does seem like a likely member but it is too bad he is like that." Puzzled, I asked, "Like what Gertrude?" She haltingly replied, "Well, you know with the ladies." This I had never heard and furthermore, I was sure that I knew the man well enough to know it was an unfair accusation. I said so to Gertrude. Her reply was, "It is not gossip because I heard from the lady whose bottom he pinched at choir rehearsal."

"Gertrude, Gertrude," I replied, "I don't think he did that and I think I can tell you who made the accusation. It was your organist, right?" Gertrude admitted I was right but I must confess I am not certain what may have happened. The man in question I am sure was not "hitting on" the organist to use a more contemporary term. But she may have come on to him, and he was just enough of a character to try to scare her off with a pinch. What I did realize was that if I had been wrong in my guess some strange thoughts might have gone through the Krauts' minds.

I wasn't universally loved, but the children were and my wife Nancy was. The children were a delight and provided us with many memorable moments and statements. Mrs. Allan tells of coming down the sidewalk where little Nancy was playing. The children called their sister "C" because they couldn't say, Nancy. On this occasion Mrs. Allan spoke to Nancy and asked her how she was. Her reply was "Reh, Bobby go to Cabbie Bible School, (Cabbie = Vacation) and leave C all alone." Mrs. Allan said it was in a most mournful tone. On another occasion we were coming out of the grocery store in Fairlee and had to descend three stairs and one of the matrons from The Ridge took Little Nancy's hand and offered to help her. The child quickly withdrew her hand and said, "C do shelf." The woman looked startled and said, "She is an independent tyke, isn't she." Of course, this was the same girl who in Maine insisted on feeding herself "C cookies."

During our first year in Orford Karl was born, on August 4, 1948. The new baby was greeted by all with enthusiasm, but little Nancy decided very emphatically that Karl was her brother. As he grew and began to play outside Nancy was always with him.

Once some older boys decided to hassle Karl and Nancy came to his defense and vigorously informed the boys, "You leave him alone. He is my brother." End of problem.

My mother and father came to visit us the first year we were in Orford. On Sunday they attended the Street Church. There the children came into the church for the first part of the service. At the second hymn they went to the sanctuary and there were two doors that led into the Sunday school rooms. Karl was among them. During the sermon one of the doors opened with a bang and Karl came through crying. Needless to say my parents were embarrassed. I couldn't explain Karl's conduct but assured my mother that Karl was well behaved and he never did anything like that before. My mother wasn't convinced. The following year they visited us again. My parents again attended church on Sunday and were hoping not to be embarrassed again. Unfortunately, they were. Karl behaved exactly as he did before. Now Nancy and I were embarrassed, as we had no explanation for Karl's conduct.

Orford was a delightful experience but Nancy and I felt it time to move on. I went to Boston to talk with the minister of the Congregational Conference, but I can't recall whether he had any churches in mind that he thought would be a good place for me to serve. He did say, however, that the Rev. Neil Hansen of the Chicago Missionary Society was in town and he thought I should talk to him. They had given Dr. Hansen an office in the same building and I was taken down the hall to meet him.

Dr. Hansen was an easy man to talk with and he had many questions concerning my ministry in

New Hampshire. He also wondered how I was able to support four children on my modest salary. I told him we got along just fine, although, we didn't have meat on the table very often. Some time later he told me my reply made a great impression on him because I wasn't complaining, just stating the facts. When I left him he said when he got back to Chicago he would give my desire to seek another parish some thought and get in touch with me.

When I returned to Orford I told Nancy of my conversation with Dr. Hansen and said, "There is a chance we might go to Chicago." She liked the idea because she had been born in Chicago. But four weeks went by and we heard nothing from Dr. Hansen. I debated what I should do and prayed for God's direction. Finally, I decided to invest in a three-cent stamp and write to Dr. Hansen.

I pointed out, perhaps unfairly, that he had aroused my interest in Chicago and that is where things ended. I would appreciate on hearing whether there were any prospective parishes there or whether I should look elsewhere. By return mail he informed me that if I was interested he wanted me to come to Chicago and the Missionary Society would pay my train fare and the necessary hotel accommodations. It seemed like a wonderful opportunity. I wanted to go and Nancy agreed that I should.

CHAPTER NINE
†
BERWYN

"The people at North Berwyn...seemed to be committed Christians and very enthusiastic about their church."

With the approval of Nancy I made the trip to Chicago to explore the opportunities in the city with Dr. Hansen. When I got to the city I learned what Dr. Hansen had in mind. He wanted me to candidate at the North Berwyn Congregational Church. It was located in Berwyn, a Chicago suburb that was largely a Bohemian community. At one time the congregation was largely German but now it was mostly Bohemian. The congregation was small but it had been growing under the leadership of Rev. Bruno Pueschel. The building was located in the middle of the block on a side street. Cab drivers had been known to argue with people and say there was no church at that location. The parsonage, on the other hand, was only two blocks away on Oak Park Avenue, which was a major thoroughfare in Berwyn.

Dr. Hansen said that if the congregation decided not to call me, he wanted me to consider becoming pastor of the Cragin Congregational Church on Chicago's north side. This church had been supported by the Missionary Society longer than any church in the society's history. The church had less than fifty members and they were all Scandinavian. The neighborhood was Italian and Polish and the Scandinavian members of the Cragin Church did not make any visitors who were not of Scandinavian background feel welcome. Their church building was also on a side street, in the middle of the block, and the sanctuary was one flight up. Any minister that accepted a call there would definitely be challenged.

I had a chance to meet the people at North Berwyn and they seemed to be committed Christians and very enthusiastic about their church. Further, Pastor Pueschell was about as high church as a Congregationalist could get. The Sunday service was quite liturgical, confirmation classes lasted one year, and at the time of confirmation the candidates wore white robes. Dr. Hansen, a most traditional Congregationalist, told me the pictures of the several confirmation groups gave him the "chills."

I don't remember my sermon on the Sunday I was a candidate, but I did receive a call from the Berwyn Church. I liked the people I met and I felt certain that God wanted me to serve Him in Berwyn. Upon my return to Orford, we gave a two weeks notice and bid "Goodbye" to the many folks we have come to love.

In January 1952, we boarded the train at Fairlee and it followed the Connecticut River to Massachusetts. There we were to change to the train bound to Chicago. In the station we were walking towards the connecting train and were passing a black porter. The children never saw anyone but white people in either Maine or New Hampshire and one of the twins in a loud voice asked me, "Is that a man?" I assured him that it was a man. When we got to Chicago they weren't surprised to find many of its citizens were black.

The Chicago Missionary Society certainly brought the clergy from New England to Chicago in grand style. Upon boarding the train for Chicago we learned that they had reserved a room big enough for the five of us. At Chicago we were met by Dr. Hansen and taken to the Palmer House, one of Chicago's finest hotels. The next day we were all taken to Berwyn to see the church and our new home. The parsonage was a two-story dwelling and eminently large for the average family. But I had not prepared Nancy for the fact that compared to the Orford house the new house was more modest. She had a moment of panic and said, "How can we get our furniture in this little house. I tried to assure her that the house wasn't little. The next question was, "Where can we put my piano?" I honestly didn't know because by that time I was seeing the house through Nancy's eyes. When the furniture came the next day we discovered the grand piano fit nicely in the front entry.

We quickly got settled and the children were enrolled in the General Custer Elementary School, which was walking distance from home. We soon learned about the Bohemian life style. The homes and yards were immaculate. The owners of a house swept the sidewalk and he swept to the middle of the street. In New Hampshire we left our Crosley station wagon with a friend and ask him to sell it for us. We shopped around for a good used car on a street in Berwyn that had scores of used car lots. We found a Ford that looked pretty good and managed to get it for a fair price. We drove it a few years and then it gave up the ghost and we sent it to the used car lot in the sky. But I felt that I had gotten my money's worth and I went back to the same car lot. Try as I could I could not get him to sell me another car. And then I was told by someone that the man had made a lot of money during the war when no cars were manufactured and he sold cars above the allowed prices under the table. Now he found it advantageous from a tax perspective simply to allow the remaining cars to depreciate. I didn't understand it, but the fact the man sold no more cars gave the story credence. It seemed that I had lucked out in getting him to sell me the Ford.

I was at a loss as to what to do and the garage where I had the Ford serviced came to the rescue. The owner said he had a Lincoln Zephyr that he would be glad to have me use. It looked like a moving scrap heap. It had only three fenders and lots of rust spots. He told me to never change the oil and if the car should stop running to take the license plates off and walk away. Actually the appearance of the car was helpful in Chicago traffic. Everyone gave me lots of room. I drove it well over a year before we found a better car that we were able to afford.

Our daughter Nancy had and probably still does have more brains that the rest of us. We went for a drive and during the trip my wife asked me to stop at a store as she wanted to go in and buy some candy for the children. She went in and came back with a large plastic bag filled with jellybeans. The children eagerly took the bag and began to inspect it. It was full of multicolored beans and then came a discovery. There was one blue jellybean. Just one. Little Nancy spoke up and said, "I want the blue jellybean." Since she spoke first I said that she could have it. The other four children protested and wanted to know why Nancy should get the blue jellybean. My answer was, "She asked first." My children informed me that it wasn't fair because Nancy would always ask first. Nobody doubted for a minutes that Nancy was the smartest and the quickest one in the family. I let her have it but I learned something that day. It wasn't a good system to decide how some of the goodies should be distributed. From that day on I made certain that all my children were treated more or less equally. I know life isn't like that but children have a right to expect some degree of equity from their parents.

The children were doing very well, except for Bobby. His twin brother, Reh, found it easier to make friends and the friends he made tended to ignore Bob. Fortunately, Custer School had two third grade classes so we asked that Reh and Bob be placed in separate rooms. It worked out very well. Bob made friends in his class and no longer needed to share Reh's friends.

Stephen was born to us in Berwyn, on September 22, 1954. We all were happy when he came, but little Nancy did cry when she heard her mother had another boy. She was so hoping for a sister. But nothing changed with the advent of Stephen. Little Nancy still ruled the roost.

We tried to fit into the neighborhood. We all took lessons in Czech and Bob and Nancy took accordion lessons. None of us turned out to be excellent linguists, but I must say, we were able to sing one Czech polka, "Julida," quite well ("Julida Julida you are my honey, Julida Julida you love me for my money"). As for the accordion, Nancy did fairly well. Bob only pursued it a year, but she continued it for five years. I gave her a dollar every time she learned a new number. Word got around and as rumors go this one got very twisted. I think it got started in a small fundamentalist church nearby. According to the rumor, Nancy was not allowed to play Polkas. I suspect it fitted in with their idea that any minister would not want his children to play any kind of dance music.

Before you say I might be mistaken, let me tell you about a child who left that church to come to our Sunday school. One day the child's mother came to talk with me and asked a few questions concerning our beliefs. She seemed satisfied with my answers and then said she would be bringing the little girl to our Sunday school. It seems that whenever she was out walking with her daughter the little girl would quickly cross run across the road that led into an alley. She had been told by her Sunday school teacher that devils lived in the alleys.

Another woman came to us from another church and asked how we felt about dancing, card playing, and movies. I told her that we had nothing against card playing, and movies needed to be chosen carefully. As for dancing I told her about our youth group and the Sunday evening worship and Bible study group. These groups danced in the church basement. She then told me that she no longer was going to another church in town because of a reply she received from a young couple to a question she asked. The church she had been going to did not allow card playing, movies, TV, or dancing. So she asked the couple, "Since you can't do those things what do you do together when go out together." The girl's answer was, "Neck." The lady told me that she wanted to be part of a church that allowed other forms of entertainment for their young people. Her problem was not unusual.

We had as neighbors a Dutch family and they had two children. When we bought a TV set the children started staying at our house when our children watched TV. Since Nancy and I knew their Reformed church did not allow their members to have or even watch television, we spoke with the children's parents. They told us they had no objection to their children watching TV in our home. It left us very baffled and confused. Of course, we monitored our children TV menu and, I guess, our neighbors just assumed that we did.

Watching our children grow up was a joy. Often we over heard things that were very enlightening. For example, we had put a rope on a branch of a tree in our yard. The children loved to climb on it and sought to get to the branch. One day the children were gathered around the rope with a group of boys from the neighborhood. One boy after another tried to reach the branch but none of them succeeded. Finally, one of the twins said, "Our sister can climb it. C show us how to do it?" Nancy quickly grab the rope and a matter of seconds reached the branch. At this point the neighborhood boys left because they had other things they would rather do.

Another time a group of children were chatting with our children and one child said his family had just purchased a new Ford. Another child said his family had a new Cadillac and a third one bragged that his family had two cars. They were all trumped when one boy from the Dutch Reformed family said, "We have four garbage trucks!" In Chicago it was the Dutch who had a monopoly on the private trash hauling business.

It was one of my children that did something which made me extremely proud.

At Christmas time it was customary for elementary school teachers to give everyone in her class a present. That's what happened in Bob's class but Reh's teacher decided to give every child an envelope with a few dollars. Reh was upset and promptly gave it back to her. When she questioned him about why, all he would say is "Money is not a Christmas present." On the way home the teacher stopped at our house and wanted Nancy and I to convince Reh that he should accept her gift. She said it was rude of Reh not to accept her gift. We told her that we didn't think Reh was trying to be rude. Reh just thought of gifts and money as two different things. We admitted his thinking was different than most children but I told her that my children are not all alike and Nancy and I just accept it as one of life's little facts. I don't know what else was said and I'm afraid Reh's teacher thought of us as uncooperative.

About this time I begin to think about my relationship with the children. There were five of

them and as a group they were a handful. Furthermore it was difficult for anyone one them to talk
with me one on one or have any individual time
with me. I decided that every week I would set aside
a day for one of my children. One of them would
have exclusive use of my time. Further they would
choose what we would do. I started with Bob and he
elected to spend the day bicycle riding. We put two
bikes on the back of the car and drove out in the
country and spent the day on our bicycles. It was a
good day, we had lunch together and covered many
miles together.

The next "Dad's day" was Reh's and he
wanted to go to the Museum of Science and Indus-
try. The museum is a child's paradise. There were
hundreds of exhibits where one could press buttons
and push levers in order to relate to the exhibit. Reh
came back all excited and all of the other children
chose the Science Museum when their day came up.
They enjoyed it and I never tired of it because it was
always a pleasure to see how they reacted to the
various exhibits from a trip in a coal mine and to a
walk through a captured German submarine. The
Chicago area had many other places that could delight adult and child alike. We went to the Chicago
Historical Society, which had a giant panorama of
the Chicago Fire, which of course the children
loved. We went to the Brookfield Zoo, the Shedd
Aquarium (that was my favorite), the Field Museum, and both of Chicago's wonderful conservato-
ries. All of these we had been to as a family together, but the children enjoyed seeing these places
again with just the two of us together.

We did the usual things that families did. When the I955 British comedy, "Belles of St. Trinians" was playing at the Capri Theater in downtown Chicago, Nancy was too busy, so I elected to take them to see it. When we got movie house, a sign at the box office said, "For Adults Only." I couldn't believe but when I asked I was told, "Yes, only adults are admitted." The children were disappointed and I checked to see what other pictures were playing and fortunately, *Jules Verne's Twenty Thousand Leagues Under the Sea* was playing not too far from where we were. That was the fare for the evening. Many weeks later "The Belles of St. Trinians" played at a different theater. I played it safe and phoned the theater and ask if children were admitted. I was told, "'Certainly." But out of curiosity I asked if they knew why the other theater a few weeks earlier restricted the movie to adults and was shocked by the answer. "Oh they just wanted to attract a large crowd."

Although I was an ordained minister in the Congregational Church, I was not a typical Congregationalist. The Congregational Church in the United States was built by the Puritans of New England, and many of their Calvinist views still prevailed in the church in the mid-twentieth century. Congregational Churches tended to be plain, almost austere, and their ministers dressed plainly.

But having been raised in the Lutheran Church, I had always valued the more high church approach, and appreciated how the wearing of vestments, a more stately church architecture, with more sacramental approach to worship could help lead a congregation to God. Thus, in my first book, *Neo-*

Congregationalism (1952), I called for a return to more liturgical forms and sacraments in Congregational worship, and along with other Congregationalists, such as Douglas Horton, constituted something of a "liturgical movement" within the church. *Neo-Congregationalism* also broached the subject of apostolic succession, and reiterated my interest in Christian mysticism.

(Many years later, in the Third Edition, I showed how these early interests of mine regarding Congregationalism led me to form the Christ Catholic Church and thought this was the direction the "true believers" should take.)

When my next book, *Theology of Congregationalism*, was published in 1957, it was a "given" in those days that Congregationalism did not have a theology. True there was no document or documents one could point to and say, "This is the theology of Congregationalism." But theology does not consist solely of documents and declarations. Obviously Congregationalists like all churches did have a theology. It was embodied in how they lived, the discipline within their churches and such acts as Holy Communion, Baptism, Marriage, and how the various congregations reacted to one another. It was in my view a mystical theology. Congregations like individuals had an awakening (birth of formation), constant discipline or purgation, revelations in the call of a minister, the liturgy they used, the covenants that they made, and the aim was Union with God. In both *Neo-Congregationalism* and *Theology of Congregationalism* I argued against the impending merger between the Congregational Christian Church with the Evangelical and Reformed Church, which I saw as an abandonment of Congregational polity (in which each congregation is independent) for a form of Presbyterianism.

While still serving as the minister at North Berwyn Congregational Church, we met Byron Reynolds, pastor of the Rosemoor Congregational Church. Byron shared my opposition to the merger and became an equal partner in the organization of the Central Association of Congregational Churches that we formed. We worked together and also socialized. One of the most memorable social occasions was a dinner at Byron's house. He invited me, Nancy, the children, and my mother-in-law and we promptly accepted. Byron was not only a good cook, but also possessed great erudition, a sense of humor, and common decency. As I recall it was a Saturday evening and we all got dressed and ready and started for Byron's house about five o'clock. It was about a ninety-minute drive so we had plenty of time for the dinner at seven o'clock. We hardly got started when Mother Taylor voiced her concern. She asked if I knew what Byron was planning to serve. I didn't and I told her so, but added he was an excellent cook.

"I'm sure he is," she replied, and then addressed the children, "Children I hope when we have dinner you will eat everything Rev. Reynolds serves. You know it is a big effort to put on a dinner for this many people and you need to show your appreciation." Someone replied, "Yes, grandmother." She then said, "That means you must clean your plates. If you are picky I will find it very embarrassing." I interjected, "I am sure they will do us proud." Mrs. Taylor's' response was, "I hope so, I truly hope so." I can remember what else was said but she didn't stop there. After a while I was feeling sorry for the children for they were getting lectured for something they hadn't done yet, and might not even do.

Byron greeted us with enthusiasm and urged us to relax in the parlor while he finished preparing dinner. We talked although the conversation seemed a bit subdued. Promptly at seven Byron invited us to the table for dinner. We came and sat down and he announced, "I hope you all like spaghetti and will like the meatballs and the sauce which is my own recipe." Mother Taylor was stunned and she tried to speak. "I, I, I eat most everything, Mr. Reynolds, but I do have, have trouble with spaghetti. I am so sorry." Always the gracious host Byron told her it was not problem he would find something else. The children were trying to suppress giggles, and Nancy and I avoided looking at one another. Byron came back with a pork chop, some lima beans, and a salad and we all set about eating and then cleaning our plates. Conversation was limited because we all did our best to suppress any laughter.

Because Nancy and I were both only children, our children did not grow up in an environment filled with aunts, uncles, nieces, nephews, and cousins. Neither did they have much contact with the older generation—the great aunts and the great uncles—which may have been beneficial. Both Nancy's relatives and mine were involved in endless disputes and feuds. I have no idea what arguments of Nancy's relatives were about, but they were often and they were fierce. So Nancy and I elected to live our lives apart. But I am so glad we did not know what went on in the rest of the family. We were on good terms with everyone but never very close. Nor did we let anything our extended family members did or said upset us.

Later in our marriage Nancy and I noticed that our children got along with one another and that such harmony in large families was not the rule, but was unusual. We attributed it to the fact that they did not observe or hear about our extended families' frequent disputes. Maybe yes, maybe no, but we never regretted not providing our children with a host of aunts and uncles. I guess ours was strictly a nuclear family.

CHAPTER TEN
†
MAYWOOD AND ITASCA

"The ducks regularly crossed the road in perfect safety because Itasca cared."

Most of my life I served the church in one way or another. After leaving seminary we went to Maine and our Congregational ministry was off to a running start. Then followed Orford and Berwyn, but the merger of the Congregational Christian Church with the Evangelical and Reformed Church in 1957 caused me to leave mainline Congregationalism the following year.

We bought a house in Maywood, a small integrated city in the western suburbs of Chicago. I found employment as an insurance agent for the Equitable Life Assurance Company. A great mistake, as the job proved to be a poor career decision. There I met Robert Childs who had worked there several years as a life insurance salesman. Bob was a congenial person and we enjoyed each other's company. I soon learned that he was not making a living at Equitable, as was the case for nearly 70 other sales people working for the same agency. After I left Equitable to work as a salesman for

117

Bremner Biscuit Company, I suggested to Bob that he do the same. While not professional jobs befitting our educational backgrounds, the jobs had the virtue of bringing in income for both of us.

Also to bring in extra income I did a lot of tutoring and had a number of tutors working with me. I went to tutor a pair of sisters, the Loveless girls, who had been victims of a horrific fire that in December of 1958 burned the Our Lady of Angels School to the ground, killing ninety-two students and three nuns, and leaving an almost an equal number with permanent injuries. Many children were burned horribly and many suffered crippling injuries from jumping out of the second and third floor windows. The Loveless girls were too disabled to go to school, and their parents had to hire a tutor to continue their education.

When summer came things got slack and I thought I could find work for the tutors by employing them as ghostwriters. I advertised that we had a ghostwriting service, and got a lot of responses. The problem was that when I talked to a respective client it was easier to do the work than to explain it to a third party what the client wanted. Bob Child was with me on this but was not a great deal of help. He was very proud of the fact that he was a Harvard graduate.

One day I saw an ad in the *Chicago Tribune* saying that, "A ghost inventor needs a ghost writer." The person placing the ad had a shop on Ashland Avenue and after phoning in response to his ad we agreed to come and speak with him and see if we could be of help to him. Now the man had a shop where he had once employed about six men. What they did was to help men and women who had jobs they couldn't handle or dead lines they could not meet. Their jobs were on the line to solve various engineering problems. The indications were that he had a successful business but it was on a decline because he had a drinking problem. In any case he expressed interest in our service, but since money was short at this time he would call us as he needed us.

Before we left he said that in addition to paying for our service, he could do something for us that no one else could. He explained that he had made an important medical discovery. He explained that it took men a long time to discover that germs caused disease. Germs he pointed out were very small. But later men discovered the virus, which was even smaller. Now he has discovered an even smaller cause of disease, so small he calls them "invisies." And he is the first one to know how to treat diseases caused by the invisies. He is an invisiologist and he could make Bob and me invisiologists. We would be among the first. I thanked him and we made a quick departure. We got into my car and started down Ashland Avenue and after a bit Bob turned to me and asked, "Do you suppose there is anything to it?" I pulled over to the curb and said, "Bob you did say you graduated from Harvard?" Well perhaps we missed a golden opportunity.

Over the years I have found several jobs for my friend, Bob Childs. I don't recall why he left Bremner Biscuit, but for a while he was looking for another job. I managed to get him another job, this time with the market research firm that my wife, Nancy, worked for. Then for a while we continued our separate ways except for that brief episode with my ghostwriting business. One day he called and sounded desperate. He and his wife had been evicted and they were sleeping at a toll way stop in their car. No job, no house, no money. "What can we do?" he asked. I suggested the only solution that came to me: "Bob, get a job as a cab driver. The tips will give you immediate cash for food, and when you get you paycheck at the end of the month you will be able to rent a place to live." "Oh, no," he said, "I couldn't do that. I haven't fall down that far." "Bob," I replied, "you are sleeping in your car on a toll road stop. What do you mean you haven't fallen down that far?" Bob wasn't listening. "Suppose some of my friends see me driving a cab?" "Suppose Bob that they see you sleeping on the toll road? Get a job as a cab driver. It's honest and it will put food on the table?" Bob didn't do it. I suspect he begged one of his relatives for help. Eventually, he went to Texas where he had a relative and he worked once again for Equitable Life. He worked there before and never made a living wage.

Young children always want to help mom and dad. Of course, when they are very little their help turns out to be more of a hindrance. But parents look forward to the day when they can be of real help. Of course then they discover that grown children are more adept than young children in avoiding work.

Each year when the children were in high school they would talk about getting a summer job. Some of our children got busy in April and May and managed to line up summer jobs. One year Reh and Bob procrastinated and when school let out they did not have a job. I had told them that this would happen if they waited until summer vacation began. But I had a job for them. Our house needed a new cesspool so as soon as school let out I got them busy digging. For two days they worked diligently and put in a good eight-hour day. I don't know where they found the time to search for a different job but on the third day of vacation they both had a job. Reh got a job at a bookbinding establishment, and Bob got a job in the mailroom of a brokerage firm. It seemed like a miracle.

Karl was always a hustler. He had a paper route in Maywood, and at one time entered a contest soliciting subscriptions for the *Chicago Tribune*. He won a bike, which was not an easy thing to do. Karl was a good talker. A friend, Fr. Kendig Cully, was visiting us one day and at one point was left alone with Karl. When Nancy came into the room and asked how they were getting along, Fr. Cully said, "Very well. Karl was talking so much I thought I could slow him down by feeding him cookies but it didn't work. He does like to talk."

My wife, Nancy, was intelligent, generous, good, and in most everything quite competent. However, in keeping house she frequently cut herself peeling potatoes, slicing meat, or doing any one of many household chores involving sharp instruments. One day she wanted to get an extra job, and she spent the day doing a job search. At the supper table she proudly announced that for a festival at Navy Pier in Chicago she had gotten a job slicing meat. Everyone at the table gasped but our daughter, Nancy said, "Dad you are not going to let her, are you?" My good wife heard and she heard the gasps, and with a good-natured smile and demeanor she said, "I guess that I am not going to slice meat." Most family decisions were made between Nancy and me. Of course, the children when they wanted something that they thought we might not sanction would asked whichever parent they thought would be more likely to give consent. But Nancy and I were usually in complete agreement and when we differed we worked it out and the children were given one answer. I don't recall any grumbling except when Karl wanted to buy a motorcycle. His mother vetoed that and, of course, I backed her up. Karl never bought a cycle. When he was old enough to do it without our consent he was mature enough not to want one.

After four years in Maywood, we discovered a house in nearby Itasca that caught my wife's eye. It was her dream house and we bought it. When we made our move all the children pitched in and one of their friends offered to help. William was a black boy about fourteen years old. We managed to haul our furniture to the new house and every one worked to get the furniture in its place and unpack many boxes. When lunch time rolled around my wife wanted to continue and suggested that I take the children to the local restaurant. It was not far from the house and we started to walk and talk about what we needed to do when we got back to the house. William was thinking and he voiced a concern that in the early 1960s was most natural. We were in an all white upper class community and planning to eat in a restaurant we had never been to before. William posed a question. "What do I do if the waitress says to me, 'We don't serve Negroes.'" My son, Karl, without any hesitation replied; "Just

tell them, William, that you don't eat Negroes."
Everybody laughed and became even more anxious
to get to the restaurant. Fortunately, the restaurant
welcomed all of us, William included. I was proud
of Karl. He had eased William's mind and expressed very vividly how we as a family stood on
the matter of racial prejudice.

We enjoyed living in Itasca, although to get
to work for Nancy and me, and to college for the
children meant an hour's ride on the Eisenhower
Expressway. I had managed to get a teaching position at Central YMCA High School. It was a school
for high school dropouts, immigrants wanting to
take English as a second language, and adults. The
age range was from seventeen to eighty-seven. In
my time there I taught English, history, and public
speaking. One of the perquisites of the job was that
my children could attend YMCA Junior College tui-
tion free. Robert immediately took advantage of it
as it was a way to get his first two years of college
at no cost.

Nancy had the summer off and thought she
might like to take some college level classes. She
realized that the high school was not challenging her
academically or holding her interest and she was
thrilled with the college. As my son, Robert put it,
"She didn't want to go back to Lake Park High for
'How can you go back to the farm once you have
seen Paree?'" At the end of the next semester, she
informed Lake Park she was leaving. When the high
school found out that she was leaving their school
for the YMCA College we received a strange phone
call. Some one from the Itasca School wanted us to
reconsider our decision to allow Nancy to transfer to

Central Y. What we were told was no one before had ever "dropped out" at Lake Park High. My wife, who had answered the phone, tried patiently to explain that our daughter was not "dropping out," but instead was "dropping in" to an opportunity. She tried to point out that Nancy was a straight A student and anxious to begin her work in college. She said she was sorry that they saw it as a mark on their escutcheon but we thought it was in Nancy's best interest.

The car was filled with Pruters who were commuting to work and school. Nancy was a librarian at the National Safety Council and the children went to the various colleges—Nancy and Robert to the YMCA Junior College, Reh the University of Illinois at Navy Pier. Karl and Stephen went to school in Itasca.

We didn't get back at the same time. I went from tutoring to the Central Y to teach, and some of the family came back by commuter train. Little Nancy often came in late and if she got off the train after a certain hour the Itasca police would pick her up and bring her home. Her mother was very amused that she had a daughter whom the police brought home several nights a week. But Itasca was a lovely place to live. On the main street there was a sign warning motorist to watch for ducks crossing. Sure enough the ducks regularly crossed the road in perfect safety, because Itasca cared.

CHAPTER ELEVEN
†
BAVARIA, BOSTON, AND ZUNI

"Boston's smallest church is large enough to meet your needs."

In 1964 I had gone to teach in Bavaria leaving the family behind in Chicago. I taught at Landerzierhung Stein not too far from Salzburg. The school was housed in an old castle built by a robber baron around the year 1000. I taught English at the seventh grade level, which was the equivalent to senior high school. It was a fun place to teach and I enjoyed the owner of the school very much, Herr Ziegler.

Herr Ziegler had some very strong ideas about eating, drinking, and music. One day a student committee came to him and asked if they couldn't have a jazz cellar. After a bit of debate he agreed to let them use the old torture chamber. "Then," he said, "The sounds that will come out will be the same as they have for a thousand years." Another committee came to him and asked that we have coffee more often. At that time we only were served coffee about three or four times a year. Herr Ziegler insisted coffee was not good for one's health, but

125

after some discussion he agreed to serve it a bit more often. His parting remark to the committee was, "I don't see why you can't be satisfied with the beer we serve. It is better for you." The school had its own brewery and its Steiner Beer was highly rated.

The school in Bavaria recruited students from the children of the new rich, the old aristocracy, and the various diplomatic corps. While I was at the school we had as a student a Hohenzollern princess, Gunila, and she was always getting weekend leave to attend various Hohenzollern parties. Then there was Prince Heinrich Reuss VII who was in his early teens and came from Austria. He had a special tutor in Latin, a French girl who said the school could never teach Heinrich Latin and she quit after one year. The director of the school said if they could teach Prince Charles in England we could find someone to teach Latin to young Heinrich. Prince Charles was regarded by many Europeans as being ten pfennig short. Before I came to the school a Hohenzollern princess was on the staff. The director was not fond of her and fired her and insisted on taking her office for his own use. So was the gossip.

While in Bavaria I bought a Prinz II, a small two-cylinder car that could do seventy miles per hour on a flat road. Anyway not being familiar with driving in Europe, when I visited Munich I was stopped by two policemen for making a left hand turn where I should not have. They informed me of my infraction of the law and wished to fine me two marks. These things were usually handled by the arresting officer on the street. Unfortunately, I only had one mark and sixty pfennig and a one hundred-mark bill. They didn't have change for the hundred and one mark sixty wouldn't do it. Very quickly after I was stopped a crowd of about twenty or thirty people had gathered. Bavarians are a nosy people and they wanted to know what was going on. In America the police would have ordered the spectators to move on. In Bavaria the spectators felt they had a right to know what was going on.

Since I did not have two marks the policeman informed me they would have to give me a ticket. Immediately the people in the crowd began to voice their objections. If I received a ticket I would have to go to city hall quickly, otherwise the fine would be ten marks. Now Bavarians have been influenced enough by the Germans to believe the law should be enforced, but in doing so the police ought to be reasonable. An argument started and one person called the policeman a *schweinhun* (pig of a dog), and after the argument continued someone else called him an animal. It went on for over twenty minutes when someone called the policeman a *pifefka* (spelling not certain but it is a Bavarian word for German, and is the equivalent of the American word "nigger"). Now I knew I was going to jail. The policemen got red and purple in his face and angrily said to the young man, "You're so smart, you figure out what to do." The young man immediately took off his hat and passed it around and collected forty pfennig, which he gave to the policeman and I gave the police my one mark and sixty pfennig. Then the most surprising thing of all happened. The policeman thanked the young man and he thanked the police officer. When the transaction was settled I drove off with a great "hurray" from the crowd. I almost decided I was not going to leave Bavaria.

In Bavaria, I discovered that there were certain gender roles in Bavarian society that was different from the United States. One role of the women was to do the snow shoveling. The men did help when their wives shoveled snow off the roof. They stood on the ground and gave directions. Whenever I met a man shoveling snow I wondered whether his wife was ill or whether he was single. It was usually one or the other. They did, however, cut wood together. The husband put it into the saw and the wife brought him the logs to cut.

In June of 1965, I left Bavaria and moved to Boston. I attended Boston University for my master's degree work in history and taught in the Boston suburbs at Dover-Sherborn High School. We settled in Pinehurst, a community populated largely by Italian-Americans. I got along with my new neighbors and made many friends among them. A year after settling there another Pruter came into the world and to my mother's dismay the baby was another boy, Maurice, born June 13, 1966, in Lowell, Massachusetts. My mother thought there were enough boys but she very quickly began to spoil the fifth boy. We named him after my favorite relative, my uncle Maurice, using the English spelling for a name pronounced "Morris."

Now Italians and the rest of us have different ways of raising children. An Italian baby is not taken out of doors in the winter and in the summer if he is taken out he is very carefully bundled up. In the coldest days of January and February we put Maurice out in the carriage to get a little nip on his cheeks. It drove our neighbors wild. Even though that winter every one on our street got bad colds, the Pruters, baby and all escaped. When Maurice would cry our neighbors would want to come and comfort him, but they were not permitted to by our German shepherd, named Dopey. One foot on our lawn was greeted with a menacing growl.

Maurice was my first bilingual child. He learned German before he learned English. One day he was playing with one of his toys and things did not go right and he was complaining aloud to himself. A visitor came through the room and asked, "Maurice, what is wrong?" He replied, "*Es ist kaput,*" and then realizing whom he was talking to Maurice added, "It is broken." Our visitor was amused by the instant translation. Maurice had a favorite toy, the record player. He had records that included Beethoven, Mozart and Yugoslavian, Bavarian, Czech, and Greek music and he could name every record. Unfortunately he didn't grow up with great musical taste. He was a happy boy.

Around this time I began my move to Old Catholicism. I had read *Episcopi Vagantes*, but it was in Bavaria and Austria in the 1960s that I had the opportunity of attending Old Catholic Churches. On my first trip to Bavaria during 1964 I was able to attend Mass in the chapel at the Mirabel Palace in Salzburg. In 1967, I made a second trip to Bavaria, and there I met Pastor Bertold Spuler and his wife in Graz. Here was a Catholicism that I could relate to. It rejected the doctrine of Papal Infallibility and he permitted priests to marry. When I returned to the States to attend Boston University, I found myself without a church home.

Congregationalism had essentially evaporated due to the merger of most of its churches with the Evangelical and Reformed Church to form the United Church of Christ. Its polity was close to Presbyterian and it became another Protestant Church and all elements of traditional Congregationalism disappeared. The few churches that did not go into the merger did not uphold traditional Congregationalism. It had been a theocratic church and most of the continuing Congregationalists thought of themselves as democratic.

In any event I went to see Archbishop Peter Zurawetzky of the Christ Catholic Church of the Americas and Europe. I was ordained a Christ Catholic priest and I was to gather a Catholic Church in the Back Bay of Boston, called the Church of the Transfiguration. The Huntington Avenue YMCA allowed us to use their beautiful chapel and we advertised in the *Boston Globe* inviting people to attend an "Old Catholic" church. We attracted members with a bit of modesty in our newspaper ads, "Boston's smallest church is large enough to meet your needs." We very quickly had a congregation of twenty to thirty people every Sunday.

We started a second parish in Deering, New Hampshire, in an outdoor chapel, which reached two summer camps. One was a Congregational camp, which had college students as counselors, and the like, and the other was a girl's riding camp. Archbishop Zurawetzky kept urging me to accept consecration as a bishop. I discussed this with the church at Boston and they suggested I accept his offer. They were unhappy with the fact that Bishop

Peter listed in the *Yearbook of Churches* that he had seventeen parishes when, in fact, the only parishes he had were in Boston and in Deering. They suggested that if he would set us apart as an independent jurisdiction I should accept Consecration. So in 1967, at Wren Oak, New York, in a chapel in the home of Bishop Uladislau Ryzy-Riski, he and Archbishop Peter consecrated me a Bishop of Boston.

In 1968, the Diocese of Boston was designated an independent, autonomous Communion, free to carry on its Old Catholic and Free Catholic traditions as Christ Catholic Church, Diocese of Boston. The new jurisdiction grew very slowly but steadily. A small parish in Hobbs, New Mexico, joined the new jurisdiction. We moved the headquarters of Christ Catholic Church to Zuni, New Mexico, in the summer of 1970. Not long after, two new parishes sprang up in Phoenix, one under the leadership of Fr. Robert Bridges and the other under the leadership of Fr. Charles Van Gorder. The latter parish was composed largely of former Mormons. Christ Catholic Church soon took a place of leadership among the Old Catholics largely because of its publishing activities. The church established the St. Willibrord Press, and it published many of the books I wrote.

My first book from the press was *Are You A Catholic Without Knowing It?* (1971), which was followed by the first edition of *The History of the Old Catholic Church* (1973), *The People of God* (1974), *One Day With God* (1991), *The Priest's Handbook* (1991), and several other titles. Our most popular title was *A Directory of Autocephalous*

Bishops, which went through many editions. Most of these titles were picked up during the 1990s by the San Bernardino-based Borgo Press, and published under the series title St. Willibrord Studies in Philosophy and Religion.

While attending Boston University for my master's degree work in history, I taught at Dover-Sherborn High School. I found it to be a real pleasure. The school was located in a highly prosperous area, in the suburbs of Boston. You could not build on less than two acres. Before I came to the school a similar town in Connecticut had a bad experience. One weekend when many parents were away the young people in their school district ran amok. The people at Dover and Sherborn felt there were too many similarities between the two school districts and they met to try to see what they could do to prevent anything happening in their towns. They felt if they had a high school that was run in a disciplined manner it might be the answer. They had Lymon B. Avery as principal. He was the right man for the right job. He called a meeting of all the parents of high school children and put before them this proposition. "You tell me what rules you want enforced and I will enforce them." They came up with a long catalogue of ideas, many of which the American Civil Liberties group would probably fight today.

Avery's dress code was considerably more rigorous than was the norm in the late 1960s. Dresses for girls and long enough to come three inches below the knee. Boys had to wear trousers (no jeans), shirt, a necktie, and either a suit coat or a sweater. Haircuts had to be acceptable to Mr. Avery, and while his standard did not require a Marine buzz cut it was most conservative in the era of "Hair." No student was permitted to come by auto. All students rode the school bus. If there was doctor's appointment and a car was needed arrangements had to be made twenty-four hours earlier with Mr. Avery. In the school the students were to be in class on time. When the bell for room change rang the students were assumed to have sufficient time to get to their next class. Mr. Avery called one of my colleagues in the office because he had observed that at the change of the bell a student in his classroom was just getting into his seat. The rule was that if a student was not in his seat ready to work he was to be sent to the office. The teacher defended himself by saying, "When the bell rang, Mr. Avery, he was getting into his seat." Mr. Avery's response was. "When the bell rings, if I am able to put a sheet of paper between the student's bottom and the seat, he is late. Further if it happens again you will be looking for another job."

Mr. Avery had no use for guardhouse lawyers. One of the teachers walked into the boys room one day and heard a toilet flush and over the stall there was a cloud of smoke. He brought the student to Mr. Avery and said the student had been smoking in the washroom. The boy defended himself with these words, "I wasn't smoking. All the teacher saw was a cloud of smoke overhead." Mr. Avery had no trouble with that. He said, "You are suspended for three days for standing in a cloud of smoke." Seems fair enough to me.

Mr. Avery was an equal opportunity disciplinarian. He was as hard with the teachers as with the students. One night, the Boston metropolitan area experienced a blackout. It was a night when a meeting was scheduled for the parents to visit the school and talk with the teachers. Everything was down. No lights and no traffic lights. Most gas stations were shut down because the pumps wouldn't work. When I arrived at the high school there were no parents there. Not a single one. But all the teachers were there. When Mr. Avery called a meeting no teacher would dare not to respond. I remember one day when the art teacher came to work and he was obviously sick. One of the teachers asked him why he came to work since he was obviously sick. His response was simple: "I was the seventh person this morning that wanted to call in sick. I knew Mr. Avery had all the sick calls he would tolerate."

Most of the teachers liked Mr. Avery. The librarian did not. She said when she came in every morning and said, "Good morning, Mr. Avery," all she ever got for a response was grunt. But she did miss Mr. Avery when he left to take another job. Always when Mr. Avery came into the library noise from student voices stopped completely. I had a reading lab on a balcony of the library and a could tell immediately when Mr. Avery entered the library, When Mr. Avery left to take another job, things changed. His successor told the students how tough he was and how the students on the Indian reservation called him, "Old Fire Eyes." Shortly after Mr. Avery left two boys got out of order and the librarian took them to the office. Shortly afterwards, "Old Fire Eyes" brought them back to the library and told the librarian he had a good talk with the boys and they promised to behave. While this was going on when the boys could be observed, the boys were laughing and making faces. That would have been unimaginable in Mr. Avery's day.

One of my students with a great deal of hesitation said he had written something for my creative writing class but he didn't know if he ought to turn it in. He said, "You might not like what I said in it." I said, "It doesn't matter I shall judge the paper on its merits." "Are you sure, Mr. Pruter?" I assured him that whatever was written I would judge on its merits. What I received was a story entitled, "Lima Bean Slavery," which was a very clever satire about our beloved principal Lyman B. Avery. I promised I would not show it to Mr. Avery and gave the student a well deserved "A."

My next teaching position was at the Goffstown, New Hampshire, junior high, which renewed my acquaintance with the laconic skin flinty New England type. At that time members of the New Hampshire legislature were paid $400 a year. They didn't stay in the state capital, Concord, long figuring out how to spend our money. It worked very well as New Hampshire was the thirty-ninth state lowest in taxation. This one year there was a proposition on the ballot to change the constitution so that legislative salaries could be raised. It was voted down four to one. When I heard the news I was anxious to talk to my neighbor to hear his reaction to it. I went next door and asked Mr. Bolton if he had heard the news. Immediately he got red and purple in the face and spoke with great anger. "I heard it and it is right. $400 a year is too much to pay a @#$%&* damn politician." I didn't ask him how he voted.

We had a lot of nice neighbors and like the rest of us they sometime had faults. One family had a son named Douglas who was Maurice's age. His father was an impatient man and often spoke to his boy in very harsh tones. One day when Maurice was playing along with his blocks and trying to build something when something went wrong he would shout "Douglas." I soon realized that Maurice thought "Douglas" was a pejorative term. He wasn't allowed to swear but "Douglas" would do. I did have a talk with his parents and I guess it did have a good effect. Maurice was well fed, had toys and records, and a grandmother that loved him. But then came Kathy, born March 26, 1968, in Manchester, New Hampshire. She was my second daughter and she was what grandmother wanted more than anything else. Unfortunately, she obviously gave her affection to Kathy, which Maurice used to get. Maurice quickly let it be known that grandmother was no longer high in his affection.

We enjoyed living in New England but felt we needed a change. In the summer of 1970, I managed to get a teaching position in Zuni, New Mexico, at Zuni High School. I was drawn to the Indian Reservation because here was living history. The Zunis more than any other Native American tribe had managed to preserve their language and their culture. Working in the region I came across a number of delightful instances of Native American interaction with the white population. A few miles north of Zuni there is a Navajo community that has a Bureau of Indian Affairs (BIA) elementary school. It is in Oak Canyon. The sign when I came to Zuni used to read Chi Chi Kiligacho Elementary School.

136

Some Navajo with a sense of humor and a dislike for pale faces must have given the name to some BIA official. What the school name on the sign said was, "The backside of a horse Elementary School." The name lasted for years since Native Americans seldom corrected anyone if they got a name wrong. Finally someone informed the BIA what it meant and it was changed to Oak Canyon Elementary School.

In Zuni, Kathy was going to become bilingual. We sent her to Head Start where ninety-five percent of the children were Zuni. She made friends and one friend in particular used invite her to dinner. I was told by the family that Kathy was making progress in Zuni. She managed to tell everyone at the table to "sit down and eat." Not polite perhaps but it was a four-word sentence.

Maurice made friends with a neighbor boy, Bernie Lasaluti. One day at the dinner table someone referred to Bernie as an Indian and Maurice objected. He insisted Bernie wasn't an Indian. I pointed out that Lasaluti was a Zuni name and that Bernie's father ran the Zuni radio program in Gallup. "But," Maurice replied, "He doesn't dance." Maurice liked to go with us to the plaza to watch the Zuni dances. To Maurice these were Indians.

He and Bernie enjoyed their times together. We had a corral in which we kept some turkeys, a pig, and a ram. The ram was named, Lincoln, and he would butt people every chance he got. Maurice suggested one day that he and Bernie go to the corral and watch the animals. Bernie was reluctant because he said, "Lincoln will butt us." Maurice said they could sit on the top of the fence where Lincoln couldn't reach them. So they went and sat on the fence. Lincoln looked at them for a while and then run up and butted the fence. When he did Bernie toppled off into the corral. Then Lincoln got him. Maurice feels bad about having urged Bernie to sit on the fence to this day.

With Maurice, Kathy and I used to go to the local Baskin-Robbins ice cream store. Normally I ordered a sugar cone with one scoop of chocolate almond and one scoop of black walnut. One day I came in and ordered a single scoop of chocolate almond and the man who was making these cones asked if I didn't want black walnut too. I told him, "No, my twin brother likes black walnut but I don't." He accepted that and from then on I played a game. I would order the chocolate and walnut cone or just the chocolate. If he offered black walnut too, I would remind him that I didn't like black walnut only my twin brother did. I would vary the order from time to time only to confuse him. It went on for six months when he said, he didn't think I had a twin brother and I had to confess. The children would often ask to go to Baskin-Robbins primarily because they got a kick out of the game.

CHAPTER TWELVE
†
Granville Avenue, Chicago

"If you want charm you go talk to Mr. Pruter. He has all the charm around here and that is what we pay him for."

Nancy and I eventually chose to live on Granville Avenue, which is on Chicago's north side. It was a pleasant neighborhood and it was made up of various ethnic groups. We had a grocery store a block away run by Greeks, a German restaurant a block away, several Irish restaurants, and an Assyrian Hall and an Assyrian Pentecostal church. And like most neighborhoods in those days, we had a local movie theater. The children by this time were grown and not living with us, so they often went to the movies when they were first released, and would come around the apartment with reports. The price in those days for first released films was about four dollars, but Nancy and I waited until they came to a local movie house, called the Bryn Mawr. Of course, when a movie came to the Bryn Mawr it had always been shown in a number of theaters for about two years. But the price was seventy~five cents. Our children couldn't understand why their parents waited two years to see a movie. Nevertheless, we waited. We saved money and we were able to carefully pick our movie so we never wasted money on one that we didn't like. Before we went to see any movie we consulted Bob. I would ask him what was playing at the Bryn Mawr and ask for his critique. If he said he liked it, Nancy and I knew we wouldn't. If he didn't like it, we knew we would. And his critique was infallible.

The one child we would see often while living on Granville Avenue was Stephen. Unlike the others, he had not yet started a family and was still going to school. Like the rest of the children he was a worker, and a student. After his graduation from University of Illinois at Chicago he decided to law school. He went to DePaul and drove a cab to get him through. Stephen always had a lot of serendipity. At one point in law school he was required to work as a law assistant. He decided he would like to work for the attorney general's office. His friends told him that would be difficult because you needed political clout to get that kind of job. But Stephen decided to apply anyway. When he went on the day for the application there were over seventy students in a room filling out applications. Now Stephen tended to stand out because of his height. At any rate, while filling out the application someone opened a door, looked in, pointed to Stephen and asked him inside to hire him.

Stephen was assigned to work with a man who did not impress Stephen much. After one day with the man Stephen resigned himself to pushing paper for the time of his internship. The second day of his internship someone else came and said they needed Stephen in another office. In that office he was assigned to a man known as "the monster." This man made the law books by his aggressive tactics, which often skirted the law. At this time, "the monster" was working on the investigation and prosecution of a number of public officials, including judges. He was successful in getting guilty verdicts against many of those he investigated. Stephen once told me it was a good experience, and he learned a lot of law, but he also pointed out that, "Much of which I learned, I never used in my practice."

Stephen graduated, got married, and joined a firm of tort lawyers. He was hired to take care of all the law cases except the tort cases. He married Eleanor who was a long time friend of both Stephen and Karl. Eleanor taught art in the public school system. She did a lot of painting and I would rate her as a good artist.

My wife Nancy occasionally got in trouble as a result of her sense of humor. She made remarks that she often regretted. The most memorable was a night at Big Mike's, a wonderful bar with a restaurant in back. It was a Serbian restaurant and we were among the few non-Serbians that went there. Nancy and I had long enjoyed the music of Yugoslavia, and the restaurant on certain nights featured a band that played the music. One rainy night we decided to go to Mike's and Nancy invited her girl friend to go with us. When we reached Mike's it was raining very hard and there was no place to park nearby so I suggested the two ladies go in and I would find a place to park and then join them. I had to park some distance away but I managed without getting too wet. When I came in there was a large group of men at the bar and when Big Mike saw me he gave me more than the usual hearty welcome.

When I arrived at the restaurant in the back Nancy was sitting a table and almost cowering. Without another word of greeting she said, "I won't every do it again." I asked her what she did and she told me in embarrassed tones while her friend had a look of bemusement. "Well." she said, "When we came in Big Mike asked me, 'Where is your husband?' and I said, 'He is at home taking care of the children,' and everyone at the bar looked as if they were going to spit on me as I hurried past to get back here in the restaurant." This was a time when Serbian men came to bars and restaurants leaving their wives home to take care of the children. It was a learning experience, which later she often talked about and was amused by it. She carefully avoided repeating anything like that again in the many subsequent nights we went out to Serbian restaurants throughout Chicago.

In the Granville neighborhood, I rented a storefront where I opened St. Willibrord Center. We divided the store into a chapel on one side and a book and card shop on the other. The sign on the door and the decorations in the window indicated what we were about. Most of the people who came to buy a card really came to ask questions. We soon found out that our storefront church answered a need for the disillusioned children of the hippie movement. Many were in their late twenties and early thirties and they had discovered that life's answer were not to be found in drugs or in the cults. They were reluctant to go to a large stone church or to a place that said, "Catholic Information Center," but they did come into the Center and they had many questions. A significant number of them had a difficult time holding a job. The hippie life did not exactly give them the discipline they needed to find and keep a job. I discovered I had talent as a job counselor. I helped hundreds of people find jobs and many I was able to help them hold jobs.

One client, I shall call Betty, proved she could find jobs, but had difficulty keeping them. I worked with her for a year, and often called her in the early morning to be sure she was ready to go to her job. She was part of the success story. Betty eventually got a job with the state welfare department and managed to earn a bachelors degree and later a master's degree in history. There were failures as well. One woman was on drugs (and probably still is) and on SSI that provided her with an apartment and income. Another young lady with a Jewish background came and was baptized in the church. She also had problems with getting and holding a job, but managed to defeat her difficulties.

When I moved from Chicago I lost contact with her, until one day I received a phone call and she said she had a problem. She was attending the Unitarian-Universalist Seminary at Chicago University and finding it difficult to adjust to her environment. She hoped to get her degree and teach at some seminary. I pointed out that it was difficult for a Jewish Catholic in a Unitarian setting. I went to Chicago and met with her and she found a group of Catholic nuns with whom she could live while in school.

As much as I loved Chicago for me it presented a difficult job situation. Nancy was happy at the National Safety Council, but I was uncertain as to what God wanted me to do. I tried a number of jobs that would provide sufficient income to help support Nancy and me, the Willibrord Center, and to provide money for whatever changes the future might have in store for us. For a year I worked in the lost prevention department of the Atlantic & Pacific Tea Stores and expected to work there for some time. Suddenly A&P decided to leave the Chicago market. For the first time in my life I found myself without a job. I was in my early sixties and not sure which way to turn. Nancy and I had purchased a house and land in the Ozarks and we knew after her retirement from the Safety Council we would be moving there.

I thought that I should develop a skill that would enable me to earn a living wherever we might be. I thought that there would always be a demand for exterminators, so I put an exterminating job high on the list in order to learn the trade. Next I noticed banks were always looking for people, not realizing that the reason for it is that they paid so little. Anyway I started out on my search and my wife and some of my children were concerned about my wanting an exterminating job and they thought it might not be good for my health. However, I didn't seem to connect with either banks or exterminators. One day I stopped in Howard Savings & Loan in Evanston and filled out an application. The next day I had a call asking me to come in for an interview. I didn't know I was about to be hired for one of the most fascinating job experiences I ever would have.

I went to Howard Savings and met Althea Prodromos who was the executive vice president and a member of the family that owned Howard Savings. The Savings company had a branch in Glenview, a nearby suburb. That branch was run by John Prodromos who was the President of the firm.

The Evanston office where I worked had seventeen employees, and from the beginning I detected a certain tenseness for which there seemed no explanation. I was given the job of Savings Counselor and had a desk and a computer in the very back. Althea's mother had a desk near me, and Althea's office was just a few steps away. I point this out because both Althea and her mother could hear what I said to the customers.

It took me only three days to learn what I needed to know to do my job. After I had mastered it I realized that there was no job description for what I was doing. I proceeded to try to put one together. As I was working on it, Althea stopped and asked me what I was doing. I told her and she immediately wanted to know if I was planning to quit. I said, "No, but I had a little extra time and thought we needed a job description for the savings counselors." She replied, "Fine but come into my office there is something I want to show you." When we went in the office she showed me a large chart she had on her desk. It outlined my salary and how it would change every other paycheck I was hired at four dollars an hour but I was to get a twenty-five cents an hour raise every other paycheck as long as I stayed with Howard Savings. The raise was retroactive to the first day I came to work for Howard, and since we were paid every two weeks, I could see that very quickly I would be reasonably well paid. She explained that she wanted to go to law school and needed someone to manage the office and she thought I could do it.

I soon learned that Althea was a most unusual person and that her idea in hiring me had many facets. There was a rumor, which soon proved true, that a large S&L, St. Paul, was planning to put a branch office in the neighborhood. Many of our customers had at one time or another clashed with Althea and openly said that when St. Paul came they would take their money there. I soon saw examples of the kind of run-in Althea had with customers. The fight would be short and bitter, and since my desk was the nearest they would stop and present me their savings certificates and ask to withdraw their money. I would let them sit by my desk and tell me their complaint. Often they would say very unflattering things about Althea and my response was never to contradict them. They would say, "Althea is a bitch." That was the most common expletive and I would agree much to their surprise. After hearing their loud complaints, which both Althea and her mother could also hear, I would talk to them about leaving their money with us. I don't recall that I failed. A few times the customer not only left his money but also added to it. The mother often re-marked that she didn't know how I did it as she had heard every word. More remarkable was that Althea heard every word. She never said anything to me about those conversations, and although we never talked about it, it was obvious that Althea felt my job was not to defend her but to placate the cus-tomer and get him to leave his money with us.

Althea was also a most generous person and never failed to reward an employee if he did something above and beyond what his job called for. For example, I had a parishioner who worked for a local weekly newspaper. I asked her to come in and interview Althea and do a feature article portraying her as a woman who successfully ran a savings and loan. When the article appeared, many of the customers saw Althea in a different light—that the manager of their savings and loan rated an article in the paper that praised her management skills.

Althea responded by sending myself, my wife, and the newspaper reporter to dine with Althea's compliments at a very fine restaurant where she was a partner. She paid for the meal, the wine, and even the tips. At Christmas time there was a bonus and a gift for my wife. She remembered Nancy at her birthday and other occasions, special or not. But most amazing to me was her knowledge of her own shortcomings and her willingness to accept them. One day she quarreled with a customer and I could hear what was being said. The customer exasperated said to Althea, "You certainly don't have any charm." The reply from Althea was very frank, "No I don't. If you want charm you go talk to Mr. Pruter. He has all the charm around here and that is what we pay him for." I guess the lady didn't want any charm that was paid for since she didn't stop to talk with me.

Althea's mother was very mystified by me. She once said to me. "I don't know how you do it. The customers come to your desk and talk about putting their money in the money markets and you tell them, 'Remember the ghost of Samuel Insull

still stalks the land'." (He built a multi-layered holding company that collapsed, causing many people to
lose large sums of money.) And she went on, "And
then when they get a certificate of deposit you ask
them, 'Whose name do you want on the account in
case you get run over by a public sanitation truck?'
And they go away smiling." A year after I left Howard Savings, I spoke with Althea and she told me
that after I left the savings counselors were instructed to use my line rather than ask "Who is the
beneficiary?" Customers found my line amusing
and the customary question about a beneficiary a bit
morbid.

When she told me this I revised my thinking
about Althea's sense of humor. I didn't give her
credit, but she showed she had one in quiet subtle
ways. I was one employee that came in on time
every single day. I also left promptly at quitting
time. Other employees tended to hang around a
while after punching the time clock. I didn't. I was
so prompt in leaving that on many occasions Althea
would stand at the door and open it for me much to
the amusement of the other employees.

Shortly after I was given the raise schedule
Althea said I needed to be an officer of the bank and
ask me what title I would like. I suggested assistant
executive vice president, which was her title. She
was not amused and asked me to choose another title. I asked her what the lowest title was that would
still make me an officer of the association. So I became the assistant corporate secretary. I chose that
title for two reasons. First, I had lived long enough
to know that titles were often given in lieu of pay
raises. Second, it seemed to be, and it turned out,

that it was easier to decline a customer who wanted an unreasonable favor, if he thought your "no" was because you didn't have sufficient authority. And it worked. Of course, there was an occasional customer who was quite astute like the one whose request I declined. He pointed to the sign on my desk that said, "Savings Counselor," and said, "I know what it says, but you run this place."

When I first was put in charge, a few of the employees had trouble grasping what had happened. I had been there a few months and one day a customer wanted to make a withdrawal and told the teller she had left her passbook at home. In those days that was a "no no." I told the teller to let her make the withdrawal and the teller told me she could not do it. At the next staff meeting Althea talked about the incident and said this to the staff, "I want all of you to understand that Mr. Pruter is in charge. If he asks you to do something you are to do it." She then turned to me and asked, "Is this what you wanted me to say?" I felt very embarrassed and said, "Yes, thank you." From then on the staff knew that the assistant corporate secretary was in charge.

I enjoyed my work at Howard Savings and felt I had made real contributions. Some were small but the big one was that I felt I had brought a different atmosphere to the institution. St. Paul Savings and Loan finally opened a branch directly across the street in the shopping mall. Not one single customer left us for St. Paul. One day a man came in and opened a new account with money he was bringing from St. Paul. After he left I took his check from St. Paul and dropped it on Althea's desk. She then told me that before St. Paul had come into the neighborhood I was the only person at Howard who was convinced we weren't going to lose money to them.

I appreciated that as much as I appreciated Althea's enthusiasm and praise concerning an advertisement I had persuaded her to place in the *Friends Journal*. One year the IRS allowed us to sell a Certificate of Deposit for ten thousand dollars that would pay interest that was tax exempt. It struck me that this would appeal to Quakers and other pacifist groups. They worry that their tax dollars will support the military and war. So our ad in the *Journal* pointed out that they could earn money and not contribute money towards war. The advertisement cost us $4.50. Since Althea had been placing ads in the Chicago paper that cost one hundred dollars and there was never a discernable benefit she readily agreed to the journal ad. We received replies from all over the country, but no deposits came our way. Since they could purchase these tax exempt certificates anywhere in the country that was not surprising. But one day we received a letter from London with a ten-thousand dollar check. A lady who lived at The Friends House not only opened the tax exempt certificate but later bought several other certificates of deposit. Althea expressed her delight and said as far as she knew we never got a deposit as the result of advertisement placed in any of the local papers. A few years after I moved to the Ozarks I visited Chicago and called on Althea and she told me that the lady in London still had money on deposit with Howard Savings & Loan.

Leaving Chicago was not easy. I was leaving a job that I loved and we were leaving family and friends behind. But we chose the Ozarks in part because it was only a day's drive from Chicago. In choosing a property in Highlandville, Missouri, we made a compromise. I wanted at least five acres of land and Nancy wanted to be where there would be people next door.

CHAPTER THIRTEEN
†
THE OZARKS

"You can't give a cat away and she sells hundreds of them for $5.00 each."

Our plans for Nancy's planned retirement from the National Safety Council were going along seemingly well. We had purchased a property in the Ozarks and Nancy would soon be drawing a Social Security check and a small pension from the Safety Council. But in March of 1982 Nancy became ill with a gall bladder attack. Of course, the doctors told her it was a simple operation and she would be in and out of the hospital in a matter of days. Shortly after the operation Nancy stopped breathing and had to be placed in the intensive care unit and the doctors were baffled as to way things had gone. On one of my visits I felt Nancy who had a sharp mind seemed quite confused. I asked her primary care physician to have a neurologist see her.

A few days went by and I was concerned and expressed my concern to Dr. Duncan Hinkson who was a personal friend of ours. Dr. Hinkson was Archbishop of the African Orthodox Church and at this time also served as head of the Chicago Medical

153

Review Board, which had the oversight of all the Chicago hospitals. He was an immigrant from the Barbados and of African descent. When I told him of my concern he said, "Let us wait until tomorrow and if they don't get a neurologist to see her, I will come up with three of the biggest, blackest, meanest looking Niggers and we'll shake that hospital up." Now Edgewater Hospital was in an all white neighborhood and I suspect Dr. Hinkson and his fellow physicians might cause the hospital some concern. As it turned out the next day the hospital neurologist saw Nancy, but was unable to determine what was causing the problem. She spent a month at Ravenswood and when she was dismissed she seemed well and everything was back on track. We were looking forward to going to Missouri in the following year.

We found an old house with a large porch in the center of downtown Highlandville and with five acres of land, and moved there in May of 1983. There were people next door and across the street. I had just gotten my second book contract from Garland Publishing Company and we opened a mail order bookstore, called Cathedral Books, and established a house of worship, the Cathedral of the Prince of Peace, by converting an old stone wash house into what became advertised as the world's smallest cathedral. We felt we had an ideal situation. But we didn't know how truly ideal it was.

We began to celebrate Mass in the Cathedral. Without any effort a small congregation began to gather. Among the first was Helen Meyer who lived across the street. She not only came, but also was baptized and confirmed as a Christ Catholic. The

154

Nemmers also came. I went to eat at Ponderosa and they greeted me and said they were going to be our next members. They did. Mrs. Nemmers was baptized and they attended regularly. We soon had a congregation of about thirty people coming from Sparta, Spokane, and Springfield. They did not all attend regularly but we could count on about eight to twelve people most Sundays. In addition we had about 3,000 visitors every year, who wanted to see the smallest cathedral in the world. Some came to pray, others came just to look and see. A number came to be married, but most of them were turned away and advised to find a church close to home where they could be part of the congregation. We definitely did not wish to become a wedding chapel.

Helen Meyer was our most interesting member. She dedicated her life to finding homes for unwanted dogs, cats, and other stray animals. People brought her unwanted animals and she would sit by the highway, Route 160, and with a sign (puppy or kitten) she would offer them to anyone who would stop. There was a very small fee but Helen often spent a great deal on the animals she offered. I knew her to spend hundreds of dollars on vet's fees for a dog that was injured and for which she later received $15.00 dollars. Kittens went for $5.00. A friend of mine was amazed because he said, "You can't give a cat away and she sells hundreds of them for $5.00 each." Her salesmanship was great. One day at a flea market she came back with 29 kittens and in three days found homes for all of them. Besides dogs and cats she sold an occasional wild duck that had been wounded and after his recovery she found a home for it. She also found a home for an emu, and after the emu craze was over a Vietnamese pig.

Meanwhile, in March of 1984, we were dealt a grievous blow. Nancy became ill and had to be hospitalized in nearby Springfield. The symptoms seemed similar to those she had in Chicago the previous year. At first a heart attack was suspected, but after many tests they concluded Nancy had sleep apnea, a relatively new term, and Parkinson's. The Springfield doctors were certain of their diagnosis but they had to have Nancy go to Little Rock, Arkansas, to get a sleep test. After a year she was able to get the tests in Springfield.

At night they put her on oxygen but during the day she got along very well. Rufus our dog became an excellent caretaker. As the sleep apnea progressed Nancy had a number of problems. Some dementia developed and she would not realize where she was. She also imagined that her mother was still alive and wanted to go down the street to her mother's house. Her mother had died in Illinois several years before we came to Chicago. Rufus detected her confusion and refused to let her out of the yard. One day I noticed that Rufus was in our Volkswagen bus and alone. It puzzled me how he got there. I let him out and thought no more about it. When it happened the next day my neighbor across the street called and said Rufus was in the bus. She explained that since Rufus would not let Nancy out of the yard, so Nancy reacted by going to the bus and calling him and letting him in the bus—because Rufus like most dogs loved to ride—and then proceeded to go down the street on her own. I of course let him out and managed to convince him that it was

all right for Nancy to go down the street. I only par-
tially convinced him. He let her go out of the yard
but he went with her always walking between her
the traffic on the street. I watched it many times and
felt confident that Rufus would give her all the help
she needed.

Some time later she developed a problem
with eye coordination due to her Parkinson's disorder. The doctor recommended that she wear a patch
over the weaker eye and rely solely on the better
eye. The children in the neighborhood were puzzled
by the patch, and one of them asked her why she
was wearing a patch over her eye. With her usual
humor Nancy said, "Haven't you heard? I have become a pirate queen?" The boy who asked replied,
"No you haven't Mrs. Pruter." The conversation
was closed with her statement, "Oh but I have."

Every year, when April came to the Ozarks,
my wife and I always purchased a season pass and
visited Silver Dollar City. The City is a theme park,
but it is built around the handicrafts of the 1890s.
They have barrel makers, glass blowers, black-
smiths, basket makers, and just about every handicraft you can think of. You can watch a man make a
chair and then, if you wish, buy it. The City also
featured a lot of entertainment. They had music
groups, both indoors and out of doors. At the ga-
zebo, just after you come in, they featured the Horse
Creek Band, which played country music, The River
Rats, who played New Orleans music, and the Cajun Connection, which was pure Cajun. One day
shortly after Rufus came to live with us we discovered that visitors were allowed to bring a pet with
you. Since Rufus was unhappy whenever we drove

off and left him we decided to see how he would do at Silver Dollar City.

If Rufus had ever dreamed of a Doggy Heaven he obviously had Silver Dollar City in mind. No sooner had we arrived we realized Rufus was a hit with many people. Not only children, but also many adults came and wanted to pet Rufus. Before the day was over, at least, a hundred people came up and asked if it was all right to pet the dog. They made a wide range of remarks, but two were repeated over and over again. "He is a beautiful dog'!" and "Boy, he sure is a big un!" Not a few women remarked that his hair is absolutely gorgeous! During our many trips to Silver Dollar City we met many men who upon coming up to Rufus to pet him would turn to their wives and remark, "Some day, I'm going to get me a big old dog like this." It wasn't any surprise to us that Rufus enjoyed the people and the fuss they made over him.

The big surprise was his reaction to the various bands. I can't remember which one he heard first, but I think it was the Horse Creek Band. We found a seat on a bench and Rufus sat in the aisle. When the first number was over and everyone applauded, Rufus barked. When the applause stopped, he stopped. Everyone was surprised and half the audience laughed. During the second number people apparently were wondering what Rufus would do when the number was over. They were not disappointed, when they applauded Rufus barked. During the entire performance Rufus gave his approval along with the audience. The first day with Rufus we listened to three bands and he reacted the same way for all of them. I also learned that he would not bark if I petted him. At one number the audience liked the performance, and began to applaud while the band was still playing. I never do that, and since I was petting Rufus I continued petting him, and he did not join the applause with his barks.

Rufus thus quickly learned when he could bark and when I did not want him to. The beauty about this way of controlling the dog was that it was not easy to detect. With one of our favorite bands, Cedric Benoit and the Cajun Connection, I used to have fun with one of its musicians, by subtly petting Rufus to keep him quiet on his solos, but lifting my hand to let Rufus bark in appreciation for his band mates' solos. The audience would of course delight in Rufus's lack of appreciation of the unhappy look-ing musician. He took it quite personally after a while. As far as Rufus was concerned his favorite group likewise was the Cajun Connection. The beat of the music was one he seemed to enjoy and then he liked to watch Terryl and Kelli do the Cajun dances.

Whenever we came to Silver Dollar City, we brought Rufus. He was more fun than anything we did, saw or heard! One of the best times we had was during the International Show. It was early in the season and Silver Dollar City brought musical groups from many nations. One group Rufus liked was Bulgarian. He seemed to like the beat of the music and would enthusiastically bark for each and every number. There was a couple behind us and after one number, the man turned to his wife and said, "That was a good number, but I don't think it was a five woofer." The Rumanian group was very pleased with Rufus and sang one song in English for him. They changed the words of a familiar American song, just a trifle. You would recognize it. It began like this, "How much is that doggy in the audience?" Rufus really gave a "four woofer" for that one.

Rufus was not a theologian. But remarkable as he was and perhaps smarter than most theologians, he was just a simple dog and was unlearned, never having been admitted into a theological seminary. But I learned some important lessons from him, nevertheless. A well known vet once said, "My dog thinks I am the most wonderful, the most powerful, the most intelligent, and the kindest being in the world, and I am not about to ask for a second opinion." Dogs are like that. Rufus loved me. He wanted not only to be with me, all of the time, but he wanted to please me. He applauded the musicians at Silver Dollar City by his barks, not just because it was fun, but also because he knew it pleased me.

It occurred to me that to Rufus I was his Master, but more than that I was his god. You are probably god to your dog also. It sounds flattering and it is. But then we are apt to say, "He is only a dog." Ponder that for a minute. Do we always want to be with God? Do we always want to please God? Does he have our absolute love, attention, and fidelity? In short, our dogs are better behaved, and more faithful to their gods, than we are to our God. No matter how you view it. No matter how you try to explain it, the dogs come out ahead. People often look down upon dogs because they will often continue to give unconditional love to a master who beats and abuses them. We, on the other hand, are asked to love the Creator who has given us life, and showers us with nothing but His Blessings. Obviously dogs are noble creatures. Forgive me if I say that Rufus was the most noble of them all.

Meanwhile, problems continued to develop with Nancy's health, for suddenly Nancy was constantly falling. Rufus came to the rescue. He would watch her carefully and when he saw she was going to fall he would quickly get between to her and place himself so that she would fall on him. One week she fell thirteen times and Rufus managed to break her fall in all but one. When he missed the one he went to her and licked her elbow. The physicians, all six of them, met and decided to take her off all medication. She was taking ten different pills and they were not certain whether one or all of them were the cause of the problem. They never found out but Nancy no longer kept falling.

Shortly after this episode the psychiatrist called in a psychologist to give her some exams to determine whether she might have Alzheimer's disease. The verdict of the psychologist was, "She doesn't have Alzheimer's; she is too sharp mentally." When Nancy was told that the tests showed she didn't have Alzheimer's, she responded and said, "I could have told you that, I don't have room for another disease."

Things did change gradually. Nancy had always wanted to do the dishes. When we had company people often offered to stay and wash the dishes but Nancy flatly refused to let them help. "Thank you" she would say, "But I want to do them." One day she said to me. "Hugo, I don't want to do the dishes anymore." That was all right with me, but I worried a bit about what it might mean. A few months later she told me she did not want to use the C-pap machine which she used every night to force her to breathe regularly. She now insisted I take the machine back to the people we rented it from. I could understand for the machine was connected to her face by a two-inch diameter hose and she had used it was several years without complaint. It didn't seem to matter as she went along without any discernable problems.

Nancy did want to do things to help others. She visited a neighbor, Mrs. Blevins, who was shut in. They would play skip-bow, their favorite card game. She also volunteered at a Century Pines, a retirement home where she went once a week to read to the residents. She usually had a dozen or more eager listeners. One morning, on July 21, 1992, she told me that she was not able to get up. I said as soon as I get dressed we should go into the hospital. While I was dressing she stopped breathing. I called 9-1-1. They told me to give artificial respiration and said the paramedics would be on the way. When they arrived they attempted resuscitation by machine and they said there was nothing further they could do. They prepared to put Nancy on a stretcher and asked that someone take the dog out. Helen offered to do so, saying "I'll get him out. Rufus knows me and he would come with me." With that Rufus laid down and it was obvious he made the decision to stay with Nancy.

I have been a pastor most of my life, and I have taught that we don't know when people die who goes to God and who doesn't. Yet, I believe that Nancy is with God. I only wish He would not have taken her so soon.

Nancy's death, unfortunately, would be followed in only a few more years by two more in my immediate family. They say the hardest thing for a parent to experience is to have a child precede them in death. This happened to me twice, first my lawyer son, Stephen, died from renal cancer at the age of forty-two, on May 11, 1998. He was followed by Hugo, a high school teacher in Brooklyn who died of colon cancer at the age of 55 on February 21, 2000. I still cannot get used to having only five children. I miss them and I miss their mother. It is a hole in my life that I shall never get used to.

My two youngest children, Maurice and Kathy, have had interesting and unusual careers. Maurice chose to finish his education in the Ozarks. He graduated from the local Spokane High School and then shortly after joined the Army. I can't explain that. He told me he thought I would be pleased. He was stationed in Bavaria and upon his release from the Army stayed in the country to study at the University of Maryland that had a branch in Munich. He elected to pursue a career in journalism and later transferred to the University of Texas in Austin, which was noted for its journalism program. While in Austin he discovered that he had a talent for stand up comedy. He soon left the university and formed several comedy groups: "Monk's Night Out" and "Squeaky Clean". He not only did well in Austin but the Motorola Corporation hired "Monk's Night Out" to many of their large corporate meetings.

Kathy chose to get her education at the University of New Mexico in Albuquerque. Upon graduation her first job was with an employment agency that recruited scientists for the Federal Government projects in Los Alamos. As a "head hunter" she did very well. However, she soon felt that just making a lot of money was not her calling and decided to train as an Occupational Therapist. When she finished her training she went to work for the Albuquerque School system. She found this work very satisfying. She has since married and her husband Daniel Abraham is a man of many talents. A lot of them connected with computers but he is also a science fiction writer and has written several novels in that genre. Dan makes the fourth writer in our family—Robert, Margaret, Daniel, and myself.

Meanwhile, after Nancy died, I was left alone with Rufus and managed the home and the Cathedral by myself. Rufus eventually died, and for companionship I got another dog. She was a German shepherd called Princess. I really yearned for human companionship, but the thought of meeting another woman and getting married did not seem likely at my advanced age. However, in 1999, about seven and one-half years after Nancy passed away, I believe that God led me to marry again. A new chapter in my life has begun.

I have served the Cathedral in Highlandville, Missouri for more than twenty years. In 2005 we moved sixteen miles away to Springfield. The property was sold to Mr. and Mrs. Larry Jackson and became an answer to our prayers. We couldn't figure how to keep maintaining the property and the expenses of the Cathedral but God did. The Jacksons are wonderful land and home developers and are building twenty houses on the old Garden of Saints trail. They have named the development "Cathedral

Estates". The Cathedral of the Prince of Peace has been rented to me for ten dollars a year for the rest of my life. The Cathedral not only gets to stay open for Sunday Mass but also will be open for the thousand plus visitors who come every year.

It is our continued hope that this pilgrimage church will always remain open for those who seek a quiet time to be with God.

Three years ago Fr. Robert O'Block and I met each other and he became another answer to prayer. The Rt. Rev. Manning of the Southern Episcopal Church gave him permission to assist me at the Cathedral and later excardinated him to our jurisdiction. Father O'Block's help has been invaluable. He also became the answer to the question, "Who shall become your successor?" In answer, in September of 2005 I consecrated him bishop in the chapel where I was hospitalized for a hip replacement.

Bishop O'Block is also a writer. He has written and published *The 7 Steps to the Cure of Souls*. His book is a clarion call for the return of traditional pastoral counseling. Christ Catholic Church in the next decade may become a leader in the return to many traditions of the first century Church.

As for me, according to my wife, I must stay around another thirty years. She is right. As I feel I am called upon to write a few more books. They are: *The History of War, Jesus, Pastoral Counseling, How to be a Husband*, a book on Meister Eckhart, and one on Hildegard of Bingen.

Please pray for us that our vision may be realized.

ABOUT THE AUTHOR

ABOUT THE AUTHOR

BISHOP KARL PRÜTER was born in 1920 in Poughkeepsie, New York. Following high school there he completed undergraduate work at Boston's Northeastern University, and then earned his master's degree in divinity at the Lutheran Theological Seminary in Philadelphia. After starting his ecclesiastical career as a congregational minister, he wrote two books, the second of which, *Neo-Congregationalism*, was later revised to include a chapter relating the personal sojourn that brought him to the Old Catholic Movement.

In 1967 Bishop Pruter was consecrated bishop of Christ Catholic Church, and the church, under his leadership, has significantly influenced the entire Old Catholic Movement. He served as presiding bishop of Christ Catholic Church from 1967 to June 1991, when he then became suffragan bishop in order to have more time to devote to spiritual writing and to promoting the retreat movement. Throughout his work in the church, Bishop Pruter has conducted literally hundreds of retreats for both Protestant and Catholic groups.

166

Along with having written scores of religious pamphlets, Bishop Pruter has also authored eight books, among them *The Teachings of the Great Mystics, A History of the Old Catholic Church, The Priest's Handbook*, and, most recently, *One Day with God* (Borgo Press, 1991), a self-instructional guide to spiritual retreats. He currently resides in Springfield, Missouri, where he serves the Cathedral of the Prince of Peace in Highlandville, which is listed in the *Guinness Book of World Records* as the planet's smallest cathedral, measuring 14 x 17 feet and seating fifteen people.

SELECTED BIBLIOGRAPHY

The Theology of Congregationalism (as Hugo R. Pruter). 1957
Neo-Congregationalism (as Hugo R. Pruter). 1958, 1960, 1973
The Teachings of the Great Mystics. 1969
A History of the Old Catholic Church (later called The Old Catholic Church [q.v.]). 1973
The People of God. 1974
The Mountain. 1979
St. Willibrord, 658-739. 1982
The Old Catholic Sourceboo (with J. Gordon Melton). 1983
Bishops Extraordinary. 1985
The Directory of Autocephalous Bishops. Issued annually in updated editions from 1985-2000, and again in 2006
The Strange Partnership of George A. McGuire and Marcus Garvey. 1986
Jewish Christians in the United States: A Bibliography. 1987
The House Church Movement. 1989
One Day with God. 1991
Prayers of a Poustinik. 1992
The Catholic Priest. 1993
The Story of Christ Catholic Church. 1993
Rufus. 1994

The Old Catholic Church: A History and Chronology,
   Second Edition. 1996
The Priest's Handbook. 1996
The Mystic Path. 1997
Live Like a Monk Outside the Walls. 1999, 2001
The Bishop's Handbook. 2005
The Blue Jellybean, Hedy Lamarr, and We Don't Eat
   Negroes. 2007